Sustainable Aquaculture for Global Food Security: Innovations, Practices, and Pathways to a Resilient Seafood Future

Copyright

Sustainable Aquaculture for Global Food Security: Innovations, Practices, and Pathways to a Resilient Seafood Future

© 2025 **Robert C. Brears**

Published by

Global Climate Solutions

ISBN (eBook): **978-1-991369-13-0**

ISBN (Paperback): **978-1-991369-14-7**

Table of Contents

Preface

The challenge of feeding a growing global population has never been more pressing. As the world faces increasing food demand, environmental pressures, and climate uncertainties, sustainable solutions for food production are essential. Traditional agricultural systems, while foundational, struggle to meet this demand due to land constraints, water scarcity, and resource-intensive practices. Simultaneously, wild fisheries are under immense strain from overexploitation and habitat degradation. In this landscape, aquaculture—when managed responsibly—emerges as a transformative force capable of delivering food security, economic stability, and ecological resilience.

Sustainable Aquaculture for Global Food Security: Innovations, Practices, and Pathways to a Resilient Seafood Future presents a comprehensive analysis of how aquaculture can evolve to become a cornerstone of sustainable food systems. This book explores cutting-edge technologies, innovative production methods, and policy frameworks that enable aquaculture to scale while minimizing environmental impacts. From recirculating aquaculture systems and integrated multi-trophic approaches to climate-adaptive farming techniques and alternative feed sources, the strategies outlined in this book demonstrate the immense potential of aquaculture to produce nutritious seafood without depleting natural resources.

Beyond technology and environmental sustainability, the book also delves into the socioeconomic dimensions of aquaculture, highlighting its role in rural development, employment generation, and global trade. By fostering responsible investment, governance, and market innovations, aquaculture can offer equitable benefits to communities while reducing dependence on overfished wild stocks.

This book is not just an exploration of current aquaculture practices; it is a roadmap for the future. It calls for a balanced approach—one that harmonizes economic growth with environmental responsibility and social equity. With contributions from industry experts, researchers, and policymakers, Sustainable Aquaculture for Global Food Security serves as an essential resource for professionals, academics, and advocates seeking to advance sustainable seafood production and build resilient global food systems.

Chapter 1. Introduction to Aquaculture and Food Security

As the global population approaches 10 billion by 2050, ensuring access to sufficient, safe, and nutritious food has become a critical challenge. Traditional food production systems, such as agriculture and wild fisheries, face mounting pressures from climate change, environmental degradation, and limited resources. In this context, aquaculture—the farming of aquatic organisms like fish, shellfish, and seaweed—has emerged as a promising solution to meet the growing demand for food.

This chapter sets the foundation for understanding aquaculture's pivotal role in addressing food security. It begins by examining the global trends in food demand and supply, highlighting the gaps that traditional systems cannot fill alone. Next, it explores the historical development of aquaculture, showcasing its evolution into a modern, sustainable industry. Finally, the chapter delves into the link between aquaculture and food security, emphasizing its potential to provide a reliable source of high-quality protein and micronutrients, particularly in regions most vulnerable to food shortages. This introduction paves the way for a deeper exploration of aquaculture's potential to transform global food systems sustainably.

1.1. Overview of Global Food Demand and Supply

Global food systems are under increasing pressure to meet the demands of a rapidly growing population while navigating the challenges of resource scarcity, environmental degradation, and climate change.

1.1.1. Growing Population and Food Needs

The global population is growing at an unprecedented pace, presenting one of the greatest challenges to food security. As of today, the world population exceeds 8 billion people and is projected to reach nearly 10 billion by 2050. This demographic surge is driven by high birth rates in developing countries, increased life expectancy due to advancements in healthcare, and urbanization trends that continue to reshape societies. These factors collectively contribute to a rising demand for food, which must grow significantly to sustain the global population. However, meeting this demand is far from straightforward.

The growth in population is not evenly distributed across regions, which exacerbates disparities in food production and consumption. While populations in many developed countries have stabilized or are experiencing slow growth, regions such as Sub-Saharan Africa and South Asia are witnessing rapid increases. These areas often have limited resources to meet the dietary needs of their growing populations, resulting in heightened risks of food insecurity and malnutrition. Moreover, urbanization in these regions places additional stress on existing food systems, as urban populations demand diverse and consistent food supplies that rural agricultural practices may struggle to deliver.

In parallel, changing dietary patterns are further compounding the strain on food systems. As incomes rise in many parts of the world, dietary preferences are shifting toward higher consumption of animal proteins, dairy, and processed foods. This shift requires significantly more resources—such as water, land, and energy—than traditional plant-based diets. The production of meat and dairy, for example, is particularly resource-intensive, and the increased demand for these foods adds further pressure on already limited agricultural capacity.

The challenges of feeding a growing population are also intertwined with environmental constraints. Land suitable for agricultural expansion is finite, and much of the available land has already been degraded by overuse, deforestation, and poor land management practices. Water resources, essential for both crop and livestock production, are also under severe strain due to over-extraction, pollution, and climate variability. These limitations highlight the need for innovative and sustainable solutions to meet the rising demand for food.

Ultimately, the growing global population and its changing dietary demands underscore the urgency of rethinking how food is produced, distributed, and consumed. Addressing this challenge will require a combination of technological innovation, policy reform, and sustainable resource management to ensure that future generations have access to sufficient and nutritious food.

1.1.2. Challenges in Traditional Agriculture and Fisheries

Traditional agriculture and fisheries, which have long been the backbone of global food production, are increasingly struggling to meet the demands of a growing and urbanizing population. These systems face a range of challenges, from environmental degradation to economic and social pressures, that threaten their ability to sustainably supply food. These challenges are compounded by the intensifying effects of climate change, which exacerbate existing vulnerabilities and create new ones.

One of the primary issues in traditional agriculture is land degradation. Overuse of arable land, combined with deforestation and poor farming practices, has led to soil erosion, loss of fertility, and desertification in many parts of the world. Fertile land is a finite resource, and its decline directly impacts the ability to produce sufficient crops. In addition, the expansion of agriculture into previously untouched ecosystems has caused significant biodiversity loss, disrupting ecological balance and reducing the resilience of food systems to external shocks.

Water scarcity is another critical challenge for agriculture. Agriculture accounts for approximately 70% of global freshwater use, and this reliance has placed enormous strain on water resources. Over-extraction of groundwater for irrigation, combined with inefficient irrigation techniques, has depleted aquifers and reduced water availability for other uses. Climate change further complicates this issue by altering precipitation patterns, leading to droughts in some areas and flooding in others, both of which disrupt crop production.

In the fisheries sector, overfishing has emerged as a significant threat to food security. Many wild fish stocks are being harvested at unsustainable levels, with some species on the brink of collapse. This overexploitation is driven by a combination of rising demand for seafood, lack of effective regulation, and illegal fishing activities. At the same time, marine ecosystems are being degraded by pollution, habitat destruction, and climate change, which affect fish populations and their ability to recover.

Both agriculture and fisheries are also heavily impacted by socio-economic factors. Small-scale farmers and fishers, who form the backbone of food production in many developing countries, often lack access to resources such as credit, technology, and markets. This limits their ability to adapt to changing conditions and reduces the overall resilience of food systems. In developed countries, large-scale industrial farming and fishing practices, while productive, often prioritize efficiency over sustainability, leading to further environmental degradation.

These interconnected challenges highlight the need for transformative changes in how food is produced and managed. Without addressing these issues, traditional agriculture and fisheries will be unable to meet the demands of a growing population in an environmentally and socially sustainable way.

1.2. Aquaculture: Definition and Historical Context

Aquaculture, the practice of cultivating aquatic organisms such as fish, shellfish, and seaweed, has evolved over centuries from small-scale subsistence methods to a vital component of modern food production systems.

1.2.1. The Evolution of Aquaculture Practices

Aquaculture has a long and varied history, evolving from ancient subsistence practices to a modern industry critical to global food security. The origins of aquaculture can be traced back thousands of years to ancient civilizations, where it emerged as a means to supplement traditional fishing and farming. Early evidence of aquaculture practices dates to around 2000 BCE in China, where freshwater ponds were used to raise carp. These early methods were simple yet effective, relying on natural ecosystems to nurture aquatic organisms. Over time, these techniques became more sophisticated, integrating knowledge of species biology and water management.

In ancient Egypt, aquaculture was similarly practiced in controlled environments, with fish being cultivated in ponds alongside the Nile River. Historical records from Rome also suggest that the Romans practiced forms of aquaculture, primarily for oysters, which were considered a delicacy. These early systems were typically small-scale and operated to meet the needs of local communities, with a focus on enhancing food availability and diversifying diets.

The Middle Ages saw limited innovation in aquaculture, as most societies relied heavily on wild fish stocks. However, certain monastic communities in Europe maintained and refined fish farming practices, using them as a sustainable source of protein during religious fasting periods. These medieval practices laid the groundwork for more organized aquaculture systems, including the use of man-made ponds and the intentional breeding of fish.

The modern era of aquaculture began in the 19th century with the advent of scientific methods and technological advancements. Researchers started to study the life cycles of aquatic species, enabling the artificial breeding and rearing of fish. Hatcheries were established to produce juvenile fish, which could then be released into natural or controlled environments for growth. This marked a significant shift from traditional methods to more intensive and scalable systems.

The second half of the 20th century saw rapid expansion and industrialization of aquaculture, driven by rising global demand for seafood and declining wild fish stocks. Technological innovations, such as recirculating aquaculture systems (RAS) and integrated multi-trophic aquaculture, further enhanced productivity and sustainability. Today, aquaculture continues to evolve, incorporating cutting-edge technologies and practices to meet the challenges of a growing population and environmental change.

1.2.2. Current Trends in Aquaculture

Aquaculture has become one of the fastest-growing food production sectors globally, driven by technological advancements, market demand, and the need for sustainable food systems. Today, aquaculture accounts for nearly half of the global fish supply, with this share expected to grow further as wild fish stocks decline. This shift underscores the increasing reliance on aquaculture to meet the nutritional needs of a growing population while alleviating pressure on natural ecosystems.

One prominent trend in aquaculture is the development of advanced production systems. Technologies such as RAS are gaining popularity due to their ability to operate in controlled environments with minimal water usage and waste generation. These systems enable year-round production, reduce the risk of disease outbreaks, and allow for farming in regions with limited water resources. Offshore aquaculture, another emerging trend, takes advantage of deeper waters to avoid coastal environmental impacts and allows for the cultivation of species in more natural conditions.

The adoption of sustainable practices is another significant trend shaping the industry. Consumers and regulators are increasingly demanding eco-friendly approaches, leading to innovations in feed development, such as the use of plant-based and insect-based alternatives to fishmeal and fish oil. Integrated multi-trophic aquaculture (IMTA), which combines the farming of multiple species to create a balanced ecosystem, is also gaining traction as a sustainable method that enhances resource efficiency and minimizes environmental impacts.

Digitalization and data-driven management are transforming aquaculture operations, enabling precision farming practices. Technologies such as sensors, artificial intelligence (AI), and big data analytics are being used to monitor water quality, optimize feeding, and predict growth rates, resulting in improved efficiency and reduced costs. Blockchain technology is also being implemented to enhance supply chain transparency, ensuring that consumers can trace the origin of aquaculture products.

Additionally, aquaculture is diversifying into new species, including seaweed and algae, which are valued for their nutritional content and role in carbon sequestration. These trends reflect the industry's ongoing efforts to adapt to global challenges and position aquaculture as a cornerstone of sustainable food systems.

1.3. Linking Aquaculture to Food Security

Aquaculture plays a pivotal role in addressing global food security by providing a sustainable and scalable source of high-quality protein and essential nutrients, particularly in regions where traditional food systems face growing challenges.

1.3.1. Aquaculture as a Contributor to Food Systems

Aquaculture has become an indispensable part of global food systems, offering a sustainable and reliable solution to the growing challenges of food security. Unlike traditional agriculture, which heavily relies on finite land and water resources, aquaculture can produce high-quality protein with a smaller environmental footprint. This efficiency is particularly vital as global demand for animal protein continues to rise, driven by population growth and changing dietary preferences.

One of aquaculture's most significant contributions to food systems is its ability to produce large quantities of nutrient-rich food. Fish, shellfish, and seaweed farmed through aquaculture provide essential vitamins, minerals, and omega-3 fatty acids that are crucial for human health. These products not only supplement diets in developed countries but also play a vital role in combating malnutrition in developing regions, where access to affordable and nutritious food is often limited. The scalability of aquaculture ensures that these benefits can reach diverse populations, bridging the gap between supply and demand in food systems.

Aquaculture also offers a solution to the overexploitation of wild fish stocks, which have been declining due to unsustainable fishing practices and environmental pressures. By farming aquatic species, aquaculture reduces the reliance on wild fisheries, allowing fish populations to recover and ecosystems to regenerate. This shift is essential for maintaining biodiversity and ensuring the long-term sustainability of marine and freshwater resources. Additionally, aquaculture can be integrated into existing agricultural systems, creating synergies that enhance overall productivity. For example, integrated fish-rice farming systems combine fish cultivation with rice paddies, improving water efficiency and nutrient cycling.

The economic benefits of aquaculture further enhance its role in food systems. The industry provides employment opportunities and supports livelihoods, particularly in coastal and rural communities. Small-scale aquaculture operations contribute to local food security by supplying fresh and affordable food to nearby markets, while larger-scale enterprises drive economic growth through exports and international trade. These economic linkages strengthen food systems by creating more resilient and interconnected networks of production and distribution.

Technological advancements have further amplified aquaculture's contribution to food systems. Innovations in breeding, feed development, and disease management have increased productivity and efficiency, ensuring a stable supply of aquaculture products. Digital tools, such as sensors and AI, enable precise monitoring and management, reducing waste and optimizing resource use. These advancements not only improve the economic viability of aquaculture but also ensure its environmental sustainability.

In sum, aquaculture's ability to produce high-quality food, alleviate pressure on wild fisheries, and create economic opportunities makes it a cornerstone of modern food systems. As the global population grows and traditional food sources face mounting challenges, aquaculture will play an increasingly critical role in ensuring food security for future generations.

1.3.2. Addressing Malnutrition and Food Accessibility

Malnutrition remains one of the most pressing global health challenges, affecting millions of people, particularly in low-income regions where access to nutritious food is limited. Aquaculture, as a rapidly growing sector of food production, offers significant potential to combat malnutrition by providing affordable and nutrient-dense food options that address both dietary deficiencies and food accessibility challenges.

Fish and other aquatic products farmed through aquaculture are among the most nutrient-rich foods available. They are high in essential vitamins and minerals, such as vitamin D, calcium, iodine, and iron, which are crucial for healthy growth and development. Additionally, fish are an excellent source of omega-3 fatty acids, which play a vital role in brain development and cardiovascular health. These nutrients are particularly critical for vulnerable populations, including pregnant women, children, and the elderly, who are most at risk of malnutrition. By making these nutrient-rich foods more widely available, aquaculture can directly contribute to improving public health outcomes.

One of the key advantages of aquaculture is its potential to produce food in regions where traditional agriculture is constrained by environmental or economic factors. In areas with limited arable land, water scarcity, or degraded soils, aquaculture can offer an alternative method of food production that does not rely on these finite resources. For example, coastal communities and small island nations can cultivate fish, shellfish, and seaweed in marine environments, providing a reliable source of nutrition where land-based farming is not feasible. Similarly, inland aquaculture systems can thrive in regions with freshwater access, creating opportunities for local food production and reducing reliance on imported goods.

Aquaculture also plays a critical role in addressing food accessibility by offering affordable options for low-income consumers. Small-scale and community-based aquaculture initiatives can supply local markets with fresh, inexpensive fish, making high-quality protein more accessible to those who may otherwise struggle to afford it. These initiatives not only enhance local food security but also empower communities by providing employment opportunities and supporting local economies. For many small-scale fish farmers, the dual benefits of producing food for personal consumption and generating income from sales create a sustainable model for addressing malnutrition.

In addition to its contributions at the local level, aquaculture supports global efforts to address food accessibility through international trade. The industry produces large quantities of fish and seafood for export, supplying regions with limited local production capacity. However, this global trade also highlights the need for equitable distribution systems to ensure that the benefits of aquaculture reach those most in need. Policies and programs aimed at reducing post-harvest losses, improving cold storage, and streamlining supply chains can enhance the accessibility of aquaculture products for underserved populations.

By integrating aquaculture into broader strategies for combating malnutrition, it is possible to bridge the gap between food production and food accessibility. Whether through localized initiatives or global distribution networks, aquaculture offers a scalable and sustainable approach to ensuring that all populations have access to the nutritious food they need for healthy and productive lives.

Chapter 2. Types of Aquaculture Systems and Practices

Aquaculture is a diverse and adaptable sector, encompassing a wide range of systems and practices tailored to different species, environments, and economic contexts. From freshwater ponds to coastal farms and high-tech offshore systems, these approaches vary in scale, complexity, and sustainability. This chapter explores the primary types of aquaculture systems, their methods of operation, and the innovative practices that are transforming the industry. By understanding these systems and their applications, we can appreciate the potential of aquaculture to meet global food demands while addressing environmental and social challenges.

2.1. Inland Aquaculture Systems

Inland aquaculture systems, which involve the cultivation of aquatic organisms in freshwater environments, are a cornerstone of global aquaculture, offering sustainable and accessible methods for producing high-quality food in land-based settings.

2.1.1. Freshwater Fish Farming

Freshwater fish farming is one of the most widely practiced forms of aquaculture, providing a critical source of protein and income for millions of people worldwide. This method involves the cultivation of fish species in freshwater environments such as ponds, reservoirs, lakes, and rivers. It is particularly prevalent in regions with abundant freshwater resources and is essential for enhancing local food security and economic development.

The primary species farmed in freshwater systems include carp, tilapia, catfish, and trout. Carp, particularly in Asia, dominate global freshwater aquaculture due to their adaptability, high growth rates, and suitability for diverse farming conditions. Tilapia, often referred to as the "aquatic chicken," is another popular choice, prized for its mild taste, nutritional value, and resilience to varying environmental conditions. Catfish farming, especially in the United States and parts of Africa, has gained significant traction due to its efficiency and market demand. Trout, known for its high nutritional content and commercial value, is predominantly farmed in cooler climates with access to clean, flowing water.

Freshwater fish farming can be classified into extensive, semi-intensive, and intensive systems, depending on the level of input and management. Extensive systems rely on natural productivity and minimal human intervention, making them cost-effective but low-yielding. Semi-intensive systems enhance natural productivity with the addition of feed and fertilizers, resulting in moderate yields suitable for small-scale farmers. Intensive systems, on the other hand, are highly controlled environments that maximize production through the use of high-quality feed, aeration, and regular monitoring. While intensive systems are more capital-intensive, they offer significantly higher yields and are common in commercial aquaculture operations.

Feed management is a critical aspect of freshwater fish farming, as it directly impacts growth rates, production efficiency, and environmental sustainability. Many farmers use formulated feeds to ensure optimal nutrition for the fish, while some also rely on natural feed sources like plankton and detritus. Balancing feed use and minimizing waste are essential for maintaining water quality and reducing the environmental footprint of farming operations.

Water quality management is another key component of successful freshwater fish farming. Parameters such as oxygen levels, temperature, pH, and ammonia concentrations must be carefully monitored and controlled to ensure healthy fish growth. Poor water quality can lead to disease outbreaks, reduced growth rates, and increased mortality, underscoring the importance of regular maintenance and monitoring.

Freshwater fish farming also offers opportunities for integration with other agricultural activities, such as rice farming or livestock rearing. Integrated systems maximize resource efficiency by recycling nutrients and utilizing by-products, creating a more sustainable and diversified farming approach. For instance, fish-rice farming involves cultivating fish in flooded rice paddies, where the fish feed on pests and fertilize the crops, enhancing productivity for both systems.

Through technological advancements and improved farming techniques, freshwater fish farming continues to evolve, addressing the growing global demand for sustainable protein sources. By enhancing yields, reducing environmental impacts, and supporting local economies, freshwater fish farming remains a vital contributor to global aquaculture and food security.

2.1.2. Integrated Multi-Trophic Aquaculture

IMTA is an innovative and sustainable approach to aquaculture that combines the cultivation of multiple species from different trophic levels within a single system. By mimicking natural ecosystem processes, IMTA creates a balanced and synergistic farming environment where the by-products of one species serve as inputs for another. This method enhances resource efficiency, reduces environmental impacts, and improves overall system productivity, making it a promising solution for sustainable aquaculture development.

At the core of IMTA is the integration of species that occupy distinct ecological roles. Typically, IMTA systems involve three main components: fed species, extractive species, and filter feeders. Fed species, such as finfish or shrimp, are provided with external feed and generate waste in the form of uneaten feed, feces, and dissolved nutrients. Extractive species, such as seaweed or macroalgae, absorb dissolved nutrients like nitrogen and phosphorus from the water, effectively reducing nutrient pollution. Filter feeders, such as mussels, clams, or oysters, consume particulate organic matter,

18

including uneaten feed and waste particles, further cleaning the water column.

One of the key benefits of IMTA is its ability to address the environmental challenges associated with traditional aquaculture. Nutrient enrichment from fish farms, often referred to as eutrophication, can harm surrounding ecosystems by depleting oxygen levels and promoting harmful algal blooms. In IMTA systems, nutrient cycling is optimized, and waste is transformed into valuable biomass by the extractive species. This not only mitigates environmental impacts but also enhances the economic value of the system by diversifying the products generated.

IMTA systems can be implemented in various aquatic environments, including marine, coastal, and freshwater settings. In coastal regions, IMTA is often practiced using open-water systems, where finfish cages are combined with nearby seaweed farms and shellfish beds. In freshwater environments, IMTA can be adapted to ponds or recirculating systems, integrating species such as tilapia, aquatic plants, and mollusks. These flexible configurations allow IMTA to be tailored to local environmental conditions and market demands.

The economic advantages of IMTA are also significant. By producing multiple species within the same system, farmers can diversify their income streams and reduce financial risks associated with market fluctuations or crop failures. Additionally, the integration of extractive species such as seaweed or shellfish can provide high-value products for food, pharmaceuticals, and biofuels, further increasing the profitability of IMTA systems.

While IMTA offers numerous benefits, its implementation requires careful planning and management. Species selection, system design, and site-specific conditions must be considered to ensure compatibility and optimal performance. Monitoring water quality, nutrient flows, and species interactions is critical for maintaining system balance and maximizing productivity.

IMTA represents a paradigm shift in aquaculture, moving away from single-species monocultures toward integrated and sustainable farming systems. By leveraging the principles of ecological balance and resource efficiency, IMTA has the potential to address the environmental, social, and economic challenges of modern aquaculture while contributing to global food security.

2.2. Coastal and Marine Aquaculture Systems

Coastal and marine aquaculture systems, which focus on cultivating aquatic species in saltwater environments, play a pivotal role in meeting global seafood demand while leveraging the vast resources of oceans and coastal areas.

2.2.1. Shrimp and Shellfish Farming

Shrimp and shellfish farming are among the most prominent and economically significant segments of coastal and marine aquaculture. These farming practices cater to the rising global demand for high-quality seafood, offering valuable protein sources while supporting livelihoods in many coastal communities. The cultivation of shrimp and shellfish has evolved significantly over the years, with advancements in technology and farming techniques aimed at increasing productivity and sustainability.

Shrimp Farming

Shrimp farming, particularly the cultivation of species like whiteleg shrimp (*Litopenaeus vannamei*) and black tiger shrimp (*Penaeus monodon*), dominates marine aquaculture in many regions. These species are highly valued in international markets due to their taste, versatility, and nutritional benefits. Shrimp farming typically occurs in coastal ponds, where water quality, temperature, and salinity are carefully managed to ensure optimal growth. Intensive farming systems, which use high stocking densities and formulated feeds, are prevalent in many parts of Asia and Latin America, the primary hubs of shrimp production.

Despite its economic importance, shrimp farming faces environmental and social challenges. Habitat destruction, particularly the conversion of mangroves into shrimp ponds, has raised concerns about biodiversity loss and ecosystem degradation. Additionally, shrimp farming operations are often associated with water pollution from nutrient-rich effluents, leading to eutrophication and degradation of surrounding coastal waters. Disease outbreaks, such as those caused by the white spot syndrome virus, are another persistent issue in shrimp aquaculture, often leading to significant economic losses for farmers.

To address these challenges, sustainable shrimp farming practices are increasingly being adopted. These include the use of biofloc technology, which promotes water quality and reduces waste through microbial communities, and RAS, which minimize environmental impacts. Certification schemes, such as those provided by the Aquaculture Stewardship Council (ASC), are also encouraging producers to adopt environmentally responsible practices and improve traceability in the shrimp supply chain.

Shellfish Farming

Shellfish farming, which involves the cultivation of species like oysters, mussels, clams, and scallops, is recognized as one of the most sustainable forms of aquaculture. Unlike shrimp farming, shellfish farming requires minimal external inputs, as these species are filter feeders that derive their nutrition from phytoplankton and organic matter in the water. This makes shellfish farming inherently low-impact and beneficial for marine ecosystems. By filtering and improving water quality, shellfish farms contribute to nutrient cycling and help mitigate the effects of coastal eutrophication.

Oyster farming is one of the most widely practiced forms of shellfish aquaculture. Oysters are typically grown on racks, bags, or longlines suspended in the water column, allowing them to filter large volumes of water as they grow. Mussels and clams are also commonly farmed using similar methods, often in intertidal or shallow subtidal zones. These shellfish species are highly valued for their taste and nutritional content, offering an excellent source of protein, omega-3 fatty acids, and essential minerals like zinc and iron.

One of the significant advantages of shellfish farming is its adaptability to different environments. From coastal lagoons to open-ocean farms, shellfish aquaculture can be implemented in diverse settings with minimal infrastructure. Furthermore, shellfish farming supports coastal livelihoods by providing stable incomes for small-scale producers and creating opportunities for eco-tourism and marine conservation initiatives.

Despite its sustainability, shellfish farming is not without challenges. Shellfish are sensitive to changes in water quality and are vulnerable to harmful algal blooms, which can render harvests unsafe for consumption. Ocean acidification, driven by climate change, poses an additional threat by affecting shell formation and growth rates. These challenges necessitate careful site selection, monitoring, and adaptive management to ensure the long-term viability of shellfish farming operations.

Shrimp and shellfish farming collectively represent vital components of coastal and marine aquaculture. While each practice has its unique characteristics and challenges, both contribute significantly to global seafood supplies and the economic stability of coastal communities. With continued innovation and a focus on sustainability, these farming methods have the potential to play an even greater role in addressing global food security challenges.

2.2.2. Seaweed and Algae Farming

Seaweed and algae farming represent some of the most rapidly expanding and sustainable sectors of coastal and marine aquaculture. These systems focus on the cultivation of macroalgae (seaweed) and microalgae for a wide range of applications, including food, feed, biofuels, pharmaceuticals, and environmental remediation. As demand for plant-based and environmentally friendly products continues to rise, seaweed and algae farming offer scalable solutions to meet global needs while providing substantial ecological and economic benefits.

Seaweed Farming

Seaweed farming involves the cultivation of various species of macroalgae, such as kelp, nori, wakame, and gracilaria, in marine environments. These species are commonly grown on ropes, nets, or other suspended structures in coastal waters. Seaweed farming is particularly prevalent in countries such as China, Indonesia, South Korea, and Japan, which dominate global production. These regions have long-standing traditions of incorporating seaweed into their diets, and the expansion of farming activities reflects both domestic and international demand.

One of the key advantages of seaweed farming is its environmental sustainability. Seaweed does not require freshwater, arable land, or external fertilizers, as it derives nutrients directly from the surrounding seawater. Additionally, seaweed cultivation acts as a carbon sink, absorbing significant amounts of carbon dioxide while releasing oxygen into the water. This makes seaweed farming a valuable tool for mitigating climate change and improving water quality in nutrient-rich coastal areas.

Seaweed farming also plays a crucial role in supporting food security. Seaweed is highly nutritious, providing essential vitamins, minerals, and dietary fiber. It is a staple ingredient in many Asian cuisines and is increasingly recognized as a superfood in Western markets. Beyond human consumption, seaweed is used as an additive in animal feed to improve livestock health and reduce methane emissions, further expanding its impact on sustainable food systems.

Algae Farming

Algae farming focuses on the cultivation of microalgae, microscopic organisms that grow in both freshwater and marine environments. Microalgae, such as spirulina and chlorella, are renowned for their high protein content and abundance of essential fatty acids, making them ideal for use in health supplements, pharmaceuticals, and biofuels. Unlike seaweed farming, algae farming often involves controlled environments, such as photobioreactors or open-pond systems, to optimize growth and productivity.

Microalgae farming is a promising solution for producing alternative proteins and bio-based products. Algae-based protein powders and oils are gaining popularity as plant-based alternatives to animal products, aligning with consumer demand for sustainable and ethical options. Furthermore, the cultivation of microalgae for biofuels offers a renewable energy source that can reduce dependency on fossil fuels, although its large-scale commercial viability is still under development.

Environmental and Economic Benefits

Both seaweed and algae farming contribute to ecosystem restoration and resilience. Seaweed farms provide habitat and shelter for marine life, enhancing biodiversity in coastal areas. Algae farming helps reduce nutrient pollution by absorbing excess nitrogen and phosphorus, preventing harmful algal blooms. These environmental benefits position seaweed and algae farming as integral components of sustainable aquaculture.

From an economic perspective, seaweed and algae farming generate employment opportunities and support coastal livelihoods. Small-scale farms supply local markets, while large-scale operations cater to global industries. As demand for sustainable products continues to grow, the economic potential of these sectors is expected to expand significantly, offering pathways for inclusive development in coastal communities.

Challenges and Future Potential

Despite its many advantages, seaweed and algae farming face challenges such as competition for coastal space, climate change impacts, and regulatory barriers. Additionally, the development of cost-effective processing and supply chain systems remains essential for unlocking the full potential of algae-based products. Continued innovation in cultivation techniques, policy support, and market development will be key to overcoming these obstacles.

Seaweed and algae farming stand at the forefront of sustainable aquaculture, offering versatile and scalable solutions to address global challenges. Their contributions to nutrition, environmental health, and economic development highlight their vital role in shaping the future of food systems.

2.3. Emerging Technologies in Aquaculture Practices

Emerging technologies are revolutionizing aquaculture practices by enhancing efficiency, sustainability, and productivity, offering innovative solutions to meet the growing global demand for seafood and aquatic products.

2.3.1. Recirculating Aquaculture Systems

RAS represent a groundbreaking approach to fish farming, utilizing advanced technology to create a controlled, closed-loop environment for aquatic species. Unlike traditional open-water or pond-based systems, RAS recycles and treats water within the system, minimizing water usage and environmental impact. This innovative method is becoming increasingly popular as a sustainable solution for producing high-quality seafood in regions with limited water resources or where environmental regulations restrict traditional farming practices.

At the core of RAS is the continuous circulation and filtration of water. The system relies on a series of mechanical, biological, and chemical processes to remove waste, maintain water quality, and provide optimal living conditions for the farmed species. Mechanical filters remove solid waste, while biological filters utilize beneficial bacteria to break down ammonia and nitrites into less harmful nitrates. Additional components, such as UV sterilizers or ozone generators, are often employed to ensure water is free from pathogens and contaminants. This highly controlled environment allows farmers to monitor and adjust parameters such as temperature, oxygen levels, and pH, ensuring optimal growth and health for the fish.

RAS is particularly suitable for high-value species such as salmon, trout, and shrimp, as well as for the production of fingerlings and juveniles for stocking in other systems. Its ability to operate year-round in any location, regardless of external environmental conditions, offers a significant advantage over traditional aquaculture methods. This makes RAS a viable option for urban areas or regions with extreme climates, where traditional farming would be unfeasible.

One of the primary benefits of RAS is its minimal environmental footprint. By recycling water and containing waste within the system, RAS significantly reduces the risk of pollution and the spread of diseases to surrounding ecosystems. The controlled nature of RAS also allows for more efficient use of feed, reducing waste and improving overall productivity. Additionally, its independence from natural water bodies minimizes the risk of escapes and genetic interbreeding with wild populations, addressing a key concern in traditional aquaculture.

However, RAS is not without challenges. The high initial investment and operational costs, particularly for energy-intensive systems, can be a barrier for many producers. Maintenance and technical expertise are also critical for ensuring the system functions effectively. Despite these challenges, ongoing advancements in technology and economies of scale are making RAS increasingly accessible and cost-effective.

RAS are shaping the future of sustainable aquaculture by combining environmental stewardship with technological innovation. Their ability to produce high-quality seafood with minimal environmental impact positions RAS as a key solution to meet the growing global demand for sustainable aquaculture practices.

2.3.2. Offshore Aquaculture Systems

Offshore aquaculture systems represent a significant advancement in the field of sustainable aquaculture, focusing on the cultivation of aquatic species in open-ocean environments away from coastal areas. These systems are designed to take advantage of the deeper waters and stronger currents found farther from shore, offering a scalable and environmentally friendly solution to meet the growing global demand for seafood. Offshore aquaculture is particularly suited for regions with limited coastal space or where nearshore aquaculture faces regulatory or environmental challenges.

One of the primary features of offshore systems is their robust design, capable of withstanding harsh ocean conditions such as strong waves, currents, and storms. These systems often consist of large, submerged cages or pens made from durable materials that ensure the containment of farmed species while minimizing environmental impacts. Advanced mooring systems anchor the cages securely to the ocean floor, allowing for stable operations even in turbulent waters. The ability to operate in deeper waters reduces competition for coastal resources and lessens conflicts with other coastal activities, such as tourism and fishing.

Offshore aquaculture systems provide several environmental benefits compared to traditional nearshore operations. The strong currents in open-ocean environments promote the natural dispersion of waste, reducing the risk of localized nutrient pollution and eutrophication. The deeper water also ensures a consistent flow of oxygen, creating optimal living conditions for the farmed species and minimizing the need for artificial aeration. Additionally, offshore systems are typically located far from sensitive coastal habitats, reducing the potential for habitat degradation and ecosystem disruption.

Species commonly farmed in offshore systems include high-value finfish such as salmon, cobia, and yellowtail, as well as shellfish like mussels and oysters. The ability to farm these species in open-ocean conditions allows for higher growth rates and improved product quality, driven by the natural flow of clean, nutrient-rich water. Offshore systems also reduce the risk of disease transmission, as the distance from shore and the constant water movement create a less hospitable environment for pathogens.

Despite their advantages, offshore aquaculture systems face challenges, including high capital costs, technical complexity, and logistical difficulties associated with remote locations. Harvesting, maintenance, and monitoring require specialized equipment and expertise, which can increase operational costs. However, ongoing innovations in automation, remote monitoring, and mooring technology are helping to overcome these barriers, making offshore systems increasingly viable for large-scale commercial operations.

Offshore aquaculture systems are paving the way for the future of sustainable seafood production. By leveraging the vast resources of the open ocean, these systems have the potential to address the limitations of nearshore farming while contributing to global food security and environmental sustainability.

Chapter 3. Environmental Sustainability in Aquaculture

Aquaculture has the potential to meet growing global food demands, but its expansion must balance productivity with environmental responsibility. Sustainable practices in aquaculture are essential to mitigate ecological impacts such as habitat degradation, pollution, and biodiversity loss while ensuring long-term viability. This chapter examines the environmental challenges associated with aquaculture and explores innovative strategies and technologies designed to enhance sustainability. From reducing waste and improving resource efficiency to restoring ecosystems, sustainable aquaculture offers pathways to protect the environment while supporting global food systems.

3.1. Environmental Impacts of Aquaculture

Aquaculture, while a vital source of food and income, poses significant environmental challenges, including habitat degradation, pollution, and impacts on biodiversity, which must be addressed to ensure its long-term sustainability.

3.1.1. Habitat Degradation and Biodiversity Loss

Aquaculture expansion, while addressing global food security needs, has contributed to significant habitat degradation and biodiversity loss in many regions. The conversion of natural habitats into aquaculture sites often disrupts ecosystems, leading to the loss of valuable ecological services and the decline of local species populations.

One of the most notable examples of habitat degradation is the destruction of mangroves for shrimp farming. Mangrove forests, which provide critical services such as coastal protection, carbon sequestration, and nurseries for marine life, have been cleared extensively in tropical and subtropical regions to establish shrimp ponds. This deforestation not only reduces biodiversity but also increases vulnerability to storm surges, flooding, and coastal erosion. The loss of mangroves affects both terrestrial and aquatic species, many of which are dependent on these habitats for survival.

Coral reef ecosystems are also impacted by aquaculture practices, particularly in regions where effluent discharge from fish and shrimp farms leads to nutrient enrichment and algal blooms. These blooms can smother coral reefs, reducing light availability and disrupting the delicate balance of reef ecosystems. Additionally, sedimentation caused by poor land management near aquaculture sites can further degrade coral habitats, affecting species that rely on these reefs for food and shelter.

In freshwater systems, aquaculture activities such as cage farming can lead to habitat degradation through nutrient accumulation and reduced water quality. Excess feed and fish waste settle on the substrate, altering the composition of benthic habitats and reducing the abundance of bottom-dwelling organisms. This, in turn, affects the broader food web, including species that rely on these organisms as a food source.

Biodiversity loss is another critical consequence of unsustainable aquaculture practices. Escapes of farmed species into the wild are a significant concern, as they can outcompete native species for resources, alter local ecosystems, and spread diseases. For example, escaped farmed salmon have been known to interbreed with wild populations, reducing genetic diversity and weakening the resilience of wild stocks. Similarly, invasive species introduced through aquaculture operations can disrupt ecosystems and threaten native biodiversity.

Disease outbreaks in aquaculture systems can also have far-reaching impacts on biodiversity. Pathogens and parasites, often exacerbated by high stocking densities and poor water quality, can spread to wild populations, causing significant declines. For instance, sea lice from salmon farms have been linked to population declines in wild salmonids in several regions, highlighting the interconnectedness of farmed and wild ecosystems.

Mitigating habitat degradation and biodiversity loss in aquaculture requires the adoption of sustainable practices and robust management strategies. Integrated site selection, which considers ecological sensitivity and habitat value, is crucial for minimizing impacts on natural ecosystems. The restoration of degraded habitats, such as mangrove replanting in former shrimp farming areas, can help rebuild biodiversity and restore ecological functions.

Technological innovations, such as closed containment systems and offshore aquaculture, offer solutions to reduce the environmental footprint of aquaculture operations. These systems minimize the risk of escapes, disease transmission, and habitat degradation while allowing for controlled production environments. Additionally, stricter regulations and certification programs, such as those provided by the ASC, encourage producers to adopt practices that prioritize environmental sustainability.

While aquaculture remains a vital component of global food systems, addressing its impacts on habitats and biodiversity is essential to ensuring its long-term viability and alignment with global conservation goals.

3.1.2. Pollution from Aquaculture Operations

Pollution from aquaculture operations represents a significant environmental challenge, particularly as the industry continues to expand to meet global food demands. The discharge of nutrients, organic matter, chemicals, and other pollutants from aquaculture farms into surrounding environments can have far-reaching impacts on water quality, ecosystems, and biodiversity. These effects are especially pronounced in areas with high densities of aquaculture operations and insufficient regulatory oversight.

One of the primary sources of pollution in aquaculture is nutrient enrichment caused by excess feed and fish waste. In open-net pen systems, uneaten feed and fish excrement accumulate in the water column and settle on the seabed. This process, known as nutrient loading, leads to elevated concentrations of nitrogen and phosphorus in the surrounding water. Excess nutrients can trigger algal blooms, including harmful algal blooms (HABs), which reduce oxygen levels in the water and create hypoxic or anoxic conditions. These "dead zones" are incapable of supporting most aquatic life, leading to declines in biodiversity and disruptions to local ecosystems.

Sediment pollution is another significant issue associated with aquaculture operations. The accumulation of organic matter beneath fish cages or other farming structures alters the physical and chemical properties of the sediment. Anaerobic conditions may develop, promoting the release of harmful gases such as methane and hydrogen sulfide, which can further degrade the environment. The impact on benthic habitats is particularly severe, as sediment pollution reduces the abundance and diversity of bottom-dwelling organisms that form the foundation of the aquatic food web.

Chemical pollution is another concern in aquaculture, as the industry frequently relies on antibiotics, pesticides, and antifouling agents to manage diseases, parasites, and biofouling. Antibiotics used to treat bacterial infections in farmed fish can enter the environment through water discharge, leading to the development of antibiotic-resistant bacteria. This poses a serious threat to public health and the efficacy of antibiotics in both human and veterinary medicine. Pesticides, such as those used to control sea lice, can harm non-target species, including crustaceans and other marine organisms, further disrupting ecosystems.

In freshwater aquaculture, pollution from pond-based systems can affect local waterways through nutrient runoff and effluent discharge. Poorly managed water exchange systems allow contaminants to enter rivers, lakes, and other water bodies, exacerbating eutrophication and impacting aquatic ecosystems. The cumulative effects of these practices are particularly concerning in regions with high concentrations of aquaculture farms, where the combined discharge from multiple operations overwhelms the natural capacity of ecosystems to absorb and process pollutants.

Closed and semi-closed aquaculture systems, while offering some advantages, are not entirely free from pollution risks. Improper management of effluents in RAS and flow-through systems can lead to the release of concentrated waste streams, which require treatment before disposal to prevent environmental harm.

Mitigating pollution from aquaculture requires the implementation of sustainable practices and advanced waste management technologies. Feeding strategies that optimize feed conversion ratios and minimize feed waste are essential for reducing nutrient loading. The use of biofilters and wastewater treatment systems in closed and semi-closed systems can help remove excess nutrients and organic matter before effluents are discharged. IMTA systems, which combine species at different trophic levels, offer a natural solution by utilizing waste from one species as a resource for another, effectively recycling nutrients within the system.

Regulatory frameworks and certification programs play a critical role in addressing pollution from aquaculture. Stringent environmental standards for effluent discharge, chemical use, and farm siting help ensure that aquaculture operations minimize their ecological footprint. Certification schemes, such as those provided by the Global Aquaculture Alliance and the Aquaculture Stewardship Council, encourage producers to adopt best practices and comply with sustainability criteria.

As aquaculture continues to grow, addressing pollution is essential to ensuring the industry's sustainability and its alignment with global environmental goals. Through innovation, regulation, and responsible practices, aquaculture can reduce its environmental impacts while contributing to global food security.

3.2. Mitigating Environmental Impacts

Mitigating the environmental impacts of aquaculture is essential to ensure its long-term sustainability, focusing on strategies that minimize resource use, reduce waste, and protect surrounding ecosystems.

3.2.1. Sustainable Feed Development

Feed development is a critical aspect of sustainable aquaculture, as feed represents one of the largest environmental and economic costs of aquaculture operations. Traditional aquaculture feeds often rely on fishmeal and fish oil, derived from wild-caught forage fish, to meet the dietary requirements of farmed species. While effective, this practice places significant pressure on wild fish populations and marine ecosystems, undermining the sustainability of the entire aquaculture sector. As a result, the development of sustainable feed alternatives has become a key focus for researchers and producers, with the aim of reducing dependence on marine resources while maintaining high growth rates and nutritional quality for farmed species.

One of the most promising approaches to sustainable feed development is the incorporation of plant-based ingredients. Soybean meal, corn gluten, and other plant-based proteins have been widely adopted as alternatives to fishmeal. These ingredients are readily available and cost-effective, making them attractive for large-scale production. However, plant-based feeds must be carefully formulated to balance essential amino acids and other nutrients that are naturally abundant in fishmeal. Advances in feed processing technology, such as extrusion and enzymatic treatments, have improved the digestibility and nutritional profile of plant-based feeds, enabling them to support the growth and health of farmed species effectively.

Another innovative solution is the use of insect-based proteins. Black soldier fly larvae, mealworms, and other insect species are rich in protein and essential nutrients, making them a highly sustainable feed ingredient. Insects can be reared on organic waste, converting food scraps and agricultural by-products into high-quality protein with minimal environmental impact. Additionally, insect farming requires significantly less land, water, and energy compared to traditional feed production, offering a scalable and environmentally friendly alternative to fishmeal. As consumer acceptance of insect-based products grows, their integration into aquaculture feeds is expected to expand.

Microalgae and single-cell proteins also show great potential for sustainable feed development. Microalgae, such as *Spirulina* and *Chlorella*, are rich in protein, omega-3 fatty acids, and other essential nutrients. They can be cultivated in controlled environments with minimal resource inputs, making them a sustainable option for aquafeeds. Single-cell proteins, derived from bacteria, yeast, or fungi, offer another innovative solution. These proteins can be produced through fermentation processes using renewable substrates, such as agricultural residues or carbon dioxide, further reducing their environmental footprint.

The use of agricultural by-products and food industry waste streams in feed formulations is another strategy to enhance sustainability. Ingredients such as rice bran, wheat middlings, and fish processing waste can be incorporated into feeds, reducing waste and creating a circular economy. These by-products often contain valuable nutrients and can be processed to improve their digestibility and nutritional value for farmed species.

While sustainable feed alternatives offer numerous environmental benefits, their adoption is not without challenges. One key issue is cost, as many alternative feed ingredients remain more expensive than traditional fishmeal and fish oil. Research and development efforts are focused on improving production efficiency and reducing costs to make sustainable feeds economically viable for producers. Another challenge is the need to tailor feed formulations to the specific dietary requirements of different species. Carnivorous fish, such as salmon and trout, have higher protein and omega-3 fatty acid requirements than herbivorous or omnivorous species, necessitating specialized feed formulations.

Regulatory frameworks and certification programs play an essential role in promoting sustainable feed development. Certification schemes, such as those provided by the ASC and the Global Aquaculture Alliance (GAA), encourage producers to adopt sustainable feed practices and provide assurance to consumers about the environmental impact of aquaculture products. These programs set standards for feed sourcing, production, and use, driving the adoption of sustainable feed alternatives across the industry.

Sustainable feed development is central to reducing the environmental impact of aquaculture and ensuring its long-term viability. By embracing innovative feed solutions and reducing reliance on wild-caught marine resources, the aquaculture industry can contribute to global food security while safeguarding marine ecosystems. Continued research, collaboration, and investment in feed innovation will be key to achieving this vision.

3.2.2. Innovations in Waste Management

Effective waste management is essential for ensuring the sustainability of aquaculture operations, as the industry generates significant amounts of organic and inorganic waste. Waste products, including uneaten feed, fish feces, and chemical residues, can contribute to nutrient pollution, water quality degradation, and habitat loss if not properly managed. Innovations in waste management are transforming the aquaculture sector, offering sustainable solutions to reduce environmental impacts while improving resource efficiency and productivity.

One of the most promising innovations in waste management is the development of integrated aquaculture systems that utilize waste as a resource. IMTA is a leading example, where the waste products of one species serve as inputs for another. In IMTA systems, fed species such as fish or shrimp produce organic waste, which is absorbed by extractive species like shellfish and seaweed. This natural recycling process reduces nutrient accumulation in the water and produces valuable secondary products, contributing to a circular economy. By mimicking ecological processes, IMTA systems effectively minimize waste and enhance overall sustainability.

RAS are another cutting-edge approach to waste management. RAS relies on closed-loop systems that continuously filter and recycle water, removing solid and dissolved waste before it is discharged. Mechanical filters, biofilters, and chemical treatments are used to remove suspended solids, convert harmful ammonia into less toxic nitrates, and sterilize water to eliminate pathogens. The concentrated waste collected in RAS systems can be further processed into fertilizer or bioenergy, creating additional value streams while minimizing environmental impacts.

Biosolid recovery and utilization technologies are also gaining traction in aquaculture. Solid waste, such as fish feces and uneaten feed, can be collected using sedimentation systems or specialized waste traps. This waste is then converted into useful products, such as compost or biogas, through anaerobic digestion or other processes. The use of biosolids as organic fertilizers supports sustainable agriculture while reducing the need for chemical inputs, creating synergies between aquaculture and terrestrial farming systems.

Technological advancements in feed management are addressing the root causes of waste generation in aquaculture. Precision feeding systems, which use sensors and automated feeders, optimize the delivery of feed to minimize waste. These systems monitor real-time fish behavior, water conditions, and feed consumption, ensuring that feed is delivered only when needed. Reducing uneaten feed not only decreases nutrient pollution but also improves cost efficiency for producers.

Biofloc technology is another innovative solution that enhances waste management in aquaculture. Biofloc systems promote the growth of microbial communities that consume organic waste and convert it into protein-rich biomass. This biomass can then be used as an additional food source for farmed species, closing the loop within the system. Biofloc technology is particularly effective in shrimp and tilapia farming, where it improves water quality, reduces the need for external feed inputs, and enhances growth rates.

Open-water aquaculture systems are increasingly incorporating waste mitigation technologies to address environmental concerns. For example, underwater cameras and sensors are used to monitor waste dispersion in real time, enabling operators to adjust feeding rates and cage positioning to minimize impacts on the surrounding ecosystem. Additionally, advanced mooring systems and cage designs reduce sediment accumulation beneath farming structures, protecting benthic habitats and promoting biodiversity.

Policy and certification initiatives are driving the adoption of waste management innovations across the aquaculture industry. Environmental regulations often require producers to implement waste treatment systems and monitor effluent discharge to ensure compliance with water quality standards. Certification programs, such as those offered by the ASC and Global GAP, set benchmarks for waste management practices, encouraging producers to adopt sustainable technologies and improve transparency in their operations.

While significant progress has been made, challenges remain in scaling up waste management innovations. High upfront costs, technical complexity, and the need for skilled labor can hinder the adoption of advanced waste treatment systems, particularly for small-scale operators. Research and development efforts are focused on reducing these barriers, making sustainable waste management solutions more accessible to producers worldwide.

Innovations in waste management are central to reducing the environmental footprint of aquaculture while enhancing its economic and ecological viability. By adopting integrated systems, leveraging advanced technologies, and aligning with regulatory frameworks, the aquaculture industry can achieve sustainable growth and contribute to global food security.

3.3. Enhancing Ecosystem Services Through Aquaculture

Aquaculture, when practiced sustainably, has the potential to enhance ecosystem services by restoring habitats, improving water quality, and supporting biodiversity while contributing to global food production.

3.3.1. Seaweed Cultivation for Carbon Sequestration

Seaweed cultivation is emerging as a critical tool in addressing climate change, primarily due to its ability to sequester carbon and mitigate greenhouse gas emissions. Seaweed, a type of macroalgae, absorbs carbon dioxide (CO_2) from the surrounding water during photosynthesis, converting it into biomass. This process not only reduces CO_2 concentrations in marine environments but also contributes to global efforts to combat climate change. As an efficient and scalable method of carbon sequestration, seaweed farming holds significant promise for enhancing ecosystem services while supporting sustainable aquaculture.

One of the key mechanisms through which seaweed contributes to carbon sequestration is the uptake of dissolved inorganic carbon from seawater. During growth, seaweed absorbs CO_2 and bicarbonates, reducing the overall acidity of the water. This process, known as ocean alkalinization, has the potential to counteract the impacts of ocean acidification caused by increased atmospheric CO_2 levels. By lowering acidity, seaweed cultivation creates a more favorable environment for marine life, particularly for calcifying organisms like corals and shellfish that are vulnerable to acidic conditions.

Seaweed's ability to sequester carbon extends beyond its growth phase. A significant portion of the organic carbon produced by seaweed is exported to the deep ocean when detached fronds sink to the seafloor. This long-term storage of carbon in marine sediments represents a natural form of carbon sequestration, removing CO_2

from the active carbon cycle. Studies suggest that well-managed seaweed farms could sequester substantial amounts of carbon annually, contributing meaningfully to global climate mitigation goals.

The scalability of seaweed cultivation further enhances its role in carbon sequestration. Unlike terrestrial plants, seaweed does not require arable land, freshwater, or chemical inputs to grow. This makes seaweed farming a sustainable and low-impact option for expanding carbon capture capacity. Coastal regions with favorable environmental conditions, such as nutrient-rich waters and suitable temperature ranges, provide ideal locations for large-scale seaweed farming. Countries with extensive coastlines, including China, Indonesia, and Norway, are leading global seaweed production efforts, demonstrating the feasibility of scaling up this practice.

In addition to its carbon sequestration benefits, seaweed cultivation provides co-benefits that enhance ecosystem services. Seaweed farms improve water quality by absorbing excess nutrients, such as nitrogen and phosphorus, from agricultural runoff or aquaculture operations. This nutrient absorption reduces the risk of harmful algal blooms and eutrophication, contributing to healthier marine ecosystems. Seaweed farms also create habitat structures that support biodiversity, offering refuge and foraging opportunities for a variety of marine species, including fish, crustaceans, and mollusks.

Seaweed's versatility extends to its applications beyond carbon sequestration. The harvested biomass can be processed into a wide range of products, including biofuels, bioplastics, animal feed, and human food. Using seaweed as a feed additive for livestock, for example, has been shown to reduce methane emissions from ruminants, further amplifying its climate benefits. Seaweed-based biofuels offer a renewable alternative to fossil fuels, reducing the carbon footprint of energy production. These applications create economic incentives for seaweed cultivation while supporting global sustainability goals.

Despite its many advantages, the implementation of seaweed farming as a carbon sequestration strategy faces challenges. One of the primary concerns is the variability in carbon sequestration efficiency across different species and environmental conditions. Factors such as growth rates, nutrient availability, and water temperature influence the amount of carbon absorbed and stored by seaweed. Additionally, the long-term stability of sequestered carbon in marine sediments requires further research to ensure its effectiveness as a climate mitigation strategy.

Regulatory frameworks and market development are also critical for scaling up seaweed cultivation. Clear policies that incentivize carbon sequestration through seaweed farming, coupled with certification programs for sustainable practices, can drive industry growth. Investment in research and development, as well as support for small-scale and community-based seaweed farms, can enhance the accessibility and scalability of this practice.

Seaweed cultivation offers a unique and promising approach to carbon sequestration, providing both environmental and economic benefits. By leveraging its ability to capture and store carbon, improve water quality, and support biodiversity, seaweed farming represents a transformative solution for addressing climate change and enhancing ecosystem services. Through continued innovation, collaboration, and policy support, seaweed cultivation has the potential to play a pivotal role in the transition to a sustainable and climate-resilient future.

3.3.2. Restorative Aquaculture Practices

Restorative aquaculture practices focus on using aquaculture as a tool to rehabilitate and enhance marine and coastal ecosystems while producing valuable resources. Unlike conventional aquaculture, which primarily aims to maximize productivity, restorative aquaculture seeks to create a net positive environmental impact. This approach integrates species and systems that actively improve water quality, restore habitats, and support biodiversity, offering a sustainable pathway for aligning food production with ecosystem health.

One of the primary examples of restorative aquaculture is the farming of bivalves such as oysters, mussels, and clams. These species are filter feeders, meaning they derive their nutrition from suspended particles in the water, including plankton and organic matter. By filtering large volumes of water, bivalves reduce turbidity, remove excess nutrients such as nitrogen and phosphorus, and improve overall water quality. This nutrient removal helps mitigate the effects of agricultural runoff and urban wastewater, preventing eutrophication and harmful algal blooms that degrade aquatic ecosystems. In areas with poor water quality, bivalve farming can play a critical role in reversing environmental degradation.

Seaweed farming is another prominent restorative aquaculture practice, contributing to ecosystem restoration through nutrient absorption and carbon sequestration. Seaweed cultivation reduces nutrient pollution by absorbing dissolved nitrogen and phosphorus, which are often responsible for coastal eutrophication. Additionally, seaweed captures carbon dioxide during photosynthesis, contributing to ocean alkalinization and mitigating the impacts of ocean acidification. Seaweed farms also provide habitat structures that support diverse marine species, enhancing local biodiversity and strengthening the ecological resilience of coastal areas.

Restorative aquaculture can also involve the creation of artificial habitats that mimic natural ecosystems, such as shellfish reefs or seagrass beds. Shellfish reefs, built using farmed or transplanted oysters and mussels, enhance habitat complexity and support a wide range of marine species. These reefs provide shelter, breeding grounds, and foraging opportunities for fish, crustaceans, and other marine organisms. Similarly, seagrass restoration projects, often integrated with seaweed farming, enhance carbon sequestration, stabilize sediments, and improve water clarity. These projects not only restore degraded habitats but also provide ecosystem services that benefit local communities and economies.

Another innovative approach to restorative aquaculture involves multi-species farming systems, such as IMTA. IMTA combines species from different trophic levels to create balanced ecosystems that recycle nutrients and minimize waste. For example, fish or shrimp farming can be paired with seaweed and shellfish cultivation, where the waste from fed species becomes a resource for extractive species. This integration reduces environmental impacts while producing diverse and valuable aquaculture products.

Restorative aquaculture also plays a critical role in rebuilding fish stocks and enhancing food security. Hatcheries and aquaculture operations can produce juveniles of threatened or overexploited species for release into the wild, supporting population recovery and ecosystem restoration. For instance, coral nurseries and reef restoration projects rely on aquaculture techniques to cultivate and reintroduce coral fragments to degraded reefs. These efforts help restore the structural complexity and biodiversity of coral reef ecosystems, which are vital for marine life and coastal protection.

Economic and social benefits are integral to the success of restorative aquaculture practices. By creating sustainable livelihoods for coastal communities, these practices align environmental restoration with economic development. Restorative aquaculture can generate income through the production of high-value seafood, eco-tourism, and ecosystem service payments, such as carbon credits or water quality improvement schemes. These incentives encourage broader adoption of restorative practices and foster long-term stewardship of marine resources.

Despite its potential, restorative aquaculture faces several challenges that must be addressed to ensure widespread implementation. Regulatory frameworks often prioritize traditional aquaculture or conservation goals, leaving limited space for integrated approaches. Financial and technical barriers, particularly for small-scale operators, can hinder the adoption of restorative practices. Additionally, the effectiveness of restorative aquaculture varies across locations and species, requiring careful site selection, monitoring, and adaptive management.

Innovations in technology and policy are crucial for scaling up restorative aquaculture. Advances in remote sensing, water quality monitoring, and ecological modeling enable better planning and management of aquaculture operations. Policies that incentivize ecosystem restoration, such as grants, subsidies, or market-based mechanisms, can encourage investment in restorative practices. Collaborative partnerships among governments, researchers, industry, and local communities are also essential for promoting knowledge exchange and fostering sustainable aquaculture development.

Restorative aquaculture offers a transformative approach to balancing food production with environmental stewardship. By enhancing water quality, restoring habitats, and supporting biodiversity, these practices create a win-win scenario for ecosystems and communities. Through continued innovation and collaboration, restorative aquaculture has the potential to address pressing environmental challenges while contributing to a sustainable and resilient future.

Chapter 4. Socioeconomic Dimensions of Aquaculture

Aquaculture is not only a critical component of global food systems but also a significant driver of economic development and social transformation. It provides livelihoods for millions of people, supports rural economies, and contributes to global trade. However, its expansion also presents challenges related to equity, resource access, and community impacts. This chapter explores the socioeconomic dimensions of aquaculture, examining its role in rural development, market opportunities, and the social challenges it faces, while highlighting its potential to promote inclusive and sustainable growth.

4.1. Role of Aquaculture in Rural Livelihoods

Aquaculture plays a vital role in supporting rural livelihoods by providing income, employment, and food security for millions of people in coastal and inland communities worldwide.

4.1.1. Employment Opportunities in Aquaculture

Aquaculture has become a significant source of employment, supporting millions of jobs globally across diverse regions and communities. The industry encompasses a wide range of roles, from farming and processing to logistics and marketing, providing opportunities for individuals with varying skill levels and expertise. As aquaculture continues to expand to meet growing global demand for seafood and aquatic products, its potential to create sustainable and inclusive employment opportunities is increasingly recognized.

Direct employment in aquaculture is primarily associated with farming operations, where workers are involved in activities such as breeding, feeding, monitoring, and harvesting. These roles are crucial for the day-to-day management of fish, shellfish, and seaweed farms and often require hands-on skills and knowledge of species-specific farming practices. Many of these jobs are concentrated in rural and coastal areas, where alternative employment opportunities may be limited. Aquaculture, therefore, serves as a vital source of income and economic stability for these communities.

In addition to direct farming jobs, aquaculture generates substantial employment in associated industries. Feed production, equipment manufacturing, and maintenance services are essential components of the aquaculture value chain, providing skilled and semi-skilled jobs. For example, workers are employed in the development and production of specialized aquaculture feeds, such as plant-based or insect-based alternatives, which require expertise in agricultural science and nutrition. Similarly, the design, production, and maintenance of aquaculture systems, including RAS and offshore cages, create opportunities for engineers, technicians, and laborers.

Processing and packaging represent another significant area of employment within the aquaculture sector. Post-harvest operations involve cleaning, filleting, freezing, and packaging of seafood products, often in facilities located near farming sites. These roles are particularly important for adding value to aquaculture products and preparing them for domestic and international markets. Processing jobs are often accessible to women, who play a vital role in the aquaculture workforce, particularly in developing countries.

The distribution and marketing of aquaculture products also create jobs across the supply chain. Workers are employed in transportation, logistics, retail, and export sectors to ensure that aquaculture products reach consumers efficiently and safely. The rise of e-commerce and online seafood markets has further expanded employment opportunities in marketing and sales, requiring skills in digital platforms and customer engagement.

Employment in aquaculture is not limited to large-scale commercial operations; small-scale and community-based aquaculture initiatives also provide significant livelihood opportunities. In many developing countries, smallholder farmers cultivate fish, shellfish, or seaweed for local markets, often integrating aquaculture with traditional agricultural practices. These operations support family incomes, improve food security, and empower marginalized groups, including women and youth. Community-based projects also create jobs in cooperative management, extension services, and training programs, fostering capacity-building and knowledge exchange.

As the aquaculture industry evolves, new technologies and innovations are reshaping its employment landscape. Advances in digitalization, automation, and AI are creating demand for skilled workers in areas such as data analysis, remote monitoring, and precision farming. For example, the use of drones and sensors for monitoring water quality and fish health requires technical expertise, while AI-driven feed optimization systems necessitate knowledge of software and analytics. These technological developments are driving a shift toward higher-skilled employment, offering opportunities for workforce upskilling and professional growth.

Despite its potential, employment in aquaculture faces challenges that must be addressed to ensure sustainability and inclusivity. Working conditions in some aquaculture operations, particularly in low-income regions, can be physically demanding and lack adequate protections. Ensuring fair wages, safe workplaces, and social protections for aquaculture workers is essential for promoting equitable employment. Additionally, addressing gender disparities and providing access to training and resources for underrepresented groups can enhance the industry's inclusivity and resilience.

Aquaculture's ability to generate employment opportunities at multiple levels of the value chain highlights its importance as an engine of rural development and economic growth. Through continued investment in technology, skills development, and social protections, the industry can expand its role as a provider of sustainable and inclusive livelihoods.

4.1.2. Women and Marginalized Communities in Aquaculture

Aquaculture plays a vital role in empowering women and marginalized communities by creating opportunities for economic participation, skill development, and social inclusion. As a rapidly growing sector, aquaculture has the potential to reduce inequalities and contribute to sustainable development by addressing the unique challenges faced by these groups. Despite this potential, structural barriers and social norms often limit the involvement of women and marginalized communities in aquaculture, necessitating targeted interventions to promote equity and inclusivity.

Women are integral to aquaculture value chains, particularly in roles such as fish processing, packaging, and marketing. In many regions, women also participate in small-scale aquaculture activities, including pond management, feeding, and harvesting. These activities provide women with an important source of income and food security, especially in rural areas where alternative livelihood opportunities are limited. Women's involvement in aquaculture not only enhances household incomes but also empowers them to make decisions about resource allocation, education, and health within their families.

Despite their contributions, women often face significant challenges in accessing resources, training, and markets. Land ownership and access to credit are key barriers that limit women's ability to establish or expand aquaculture operations. Traditional gender roles and societal norms further restrict women's participation in decision-making processes within the sector. Addressing these barriers requires policies and programs that promote gender equality, such as providing women with access to microfinance, capacity-building initiatives, and technical training tailored to their needs.

Marginalized communities, including indigenous groups, ethnic minorities, and low-income households, also benefit significantly from aquaculture. Small-scale and community-based aquaculture initiatives are particularly effective in reaching these groups, providing them with opportunities to improve their livelihoods and escape poverty. In many cases, aquaculture serves as a viable alternative to traditional livelihoods that may be threatened by environmental degradation, overfishing, or climate change. For example, seaweed and shellfish farming projects in coastal areas often target marginalized communities, enabling them to leverage local resources and traditional knowledge to generate income and enhance food security.

However, these communities also face unique challenges in participating fully in aquaculture. Limited access to technology, infrastructure, and training can hinder their ability to adopt modern aquaculture practices and compete in larger markets. Additionally, geographic isolation and lack of representation in policy-making processes often leave marginalized communities excluded from decisions that affect their livelihoods. Strengthening support systems for these groups, such as cooperative models and partnerships with non-governmental organizations, can help bridge these gaps and ensure their inclusion in the sector.

Efforts to empower women and marginalized communities in aquaculture are increasingly being integrated into global development strategies. International organizations, governments, and industry stakeholders are recognizing the importance of inclusivity in fostering sustainable growth. Initiatives such as the Gender in Aquaculture and Fisheries program (GAF) and targeted capacity-building projects aim to address gender and social inequalities, creating pathways for underrepresented groups to participate in and benefit from aquaculture.

Technology and innovation also play a critical role in enhancing inclusivity in aquaculture. Digital tools, such as mobile applications for market access or online training platforms, can overcome barriers related to geographic isolation and limited resources. These tools enable women and marginalized communities to acquire knowledge, connect with buyers, and improve their practices, thereby enhancing their economic resilience.

By addressing structural barriers and promoting equitable access to resources and opportunities, aquaculture can become a powerful tool for empowering women and marginalized communities. Their active participation not only strengthens the sector's resilience but also contributes to broader societal goals of gender equality and social inclusion.

4.2. Economic Benefits and Market Opportunities

Aquaculture offers significant economic benefits and market opportunities, driving global trade, supporting local economies, and meeting the growing demand for sustainable seafood and aquatic products.

4.2.1. Global Trade and Export Potential of Aquaculture Products

Aquaculture has emerged as a key driver of global seafood trade, providing a growing share of the fish and aquatic products consumed worldwide. As wild fish stocks face increasing pressure and consumer demand for seafood rises, aquaculture has become the cornerstone of global fish supply, accounting for nearly half of all seafood production. This shift has created significant export opportunities for aquaculture-producing countries, enabling them to capitalize on international markets while contributing to economic growth and food security.

The global trade in aquaculture products encompasses a wide range of species, including finfish, shellfish, crustaceans, and seaweed. High-value species such as salmon, shrimp, and tuna dominate international exports due to their strong consumer demand in premium markets. For example, farmed Atlantic salmon is a leading aquaculture export, with Norway, Chile, and Canada among the top exporters. Similarly, shrimp farming has become a major economic activity in countries such as India, Ecuador, and Vietnam, which supply frozen and processed shrimp to markets in North America, Europe, and Asia.

Emerging markets for aquaculture products are also growing rapidly, driven by shifting dietary patterns and rising incomes in developing regions. In Asia, for instance, increasing urbanization and a growing middle class have fueled demand for high-quality seafood, creating new opportunities for exporters. The expansion of trade networks and regional free trade agreements further facilitates access to these markets, allowing aquaculture producers to diversify their export destinations and reduce reliance on traditional buyers.

The export potential of aquaculture is bolstered by advancements in processing and packaging technologies, which enable products to maintain freshness and quality during transportation. Innovations such as vacuum-sealing, freezing, and modified atmosphere packaging have extended the shelf life of aquaculture products, ensuring that they meet the stringent quality standards of international markets. Additionally, value-added processing, such as filleting, breading, or ready-to-eat packaging, enhances the appeal of aquaculture products and increases their market value.

Sustainability and certification play an increasingly important role in the global trade of aquaculture products. Consumers and retailers in major markets demand assurances that seafood is produced in an environmentally responsible and socially equitable manner. Certification programs such as those offered by the ASC and Global GAP provide transparency and credibility, enabling producers to access high-value markets and differentiate their products. These certifications not only drive export potential but also encourage the adoption of sustainable practices across the industry.

While global trade in aquaculture products offers significant economic benefits, it also presents challenges that must be addressed to ensure long-term success. Trade barriers, including tariffs, non-tariff measures, and stringent import regulations, can limit market access for some producers. Developing countries, in particular, often face difficulties meeting the food safety and quality standards required by importing nations. Investments in infrastructure, capacity-building, and regulatory compliance are critical to overcoming these obstacles and enabling producers to compete effectively in international markets.

Logistics and transportation are other critical factors influencing the export potential of aquaculture products. The perishable nature of seafood requires efficient cold chain systems to maintain product quality from farm to consumer. Delays or disruptions in transportation can result in significant economic losses, underscoring the need for robust logistics networks and contingency planning. Technological advancements, such as real-time tracking and blockchain, are increasingly being used to enhance supply chain transparency and efficiency.

Global trade in aquaculture products also has socio-economic implications for producing countries. Export-oriented aquaculture operations create employment opportunities, generate foreign exchange earnings, and contribute to rural development. Small-scale producers, however, may struggle to participate in export markets due to limited resources and access to international buyers. Support mechanisms such as cooperatives, market linkages, and fair trade initiatives can help smallholders benefit from global trade and ensure that the economic gains from aquaculture are equitably distributed.

The export potential of aquaculture products underscores the industry's role as a key contributor to global food security and economic development. As demand for seafood continues to grow, the trade in aquaculture products will remain a critical driver of industry expansion and a valuable opportunity for producers worldwide.

4.2.2. Domestic Market Growth for Aquaculture

The domestic market for aquaculture products has been expanding rapidly, driven by increasing consumer demand for high-quality, sustainable, and locally produced seafood. As populations grow and dietary preferences shift toward healthier and protein-rich foods, aquaculture has emerged as a reliable source to meet domestic consumption needs. This growth not only supports local economies but also reduces dependence on imported seafood, fostering self-sufficiency in food production.

One of the key drivers of domestic market growth in aquaculture is the rising awareness of the health benefits associated with seafood consumption. Fish and other aquatic products are recognized for their high protein content, omega-3 fatty acids, and essential vitamins and minerals. These attributes appeal to health-conscious consumers, who are incorporating more seafood into their diets. Additionally, the growing prevalence of plant-based and flexitarian diets has increased the popularity of seaweed and other aquaculture-derived products as sustainable and nutritious food options.

Urbanization and income growth in developing countries have also fueled domestic demand for aquaculture products. As urban populations expand, so does the demand for convenient, affordable, and diverse food options. Aquaculture provides an accessible source of fresh and processed seafood, catering to the dietary needs of urban consumers. Furthermore, higher disposable incomes enable households to spend more on premium seafood products, such as shrimp, salmon, and shellfish, boosting the domestic market for high-value aquaculture species.

In many countries, government policies and initiatives play a pivotal role in promoting domestic aquaculture markets. Subsidies, financial incentives, and technical assistance for aquaculture farmers have contributed to the sector's growth and improved its competitiveness against imported products. Public awareness campaigns highlighting the benefits of consuming locally produced seafood also encourage consumers to support domestic aquaculture industries. These efforts not only stimulate market demand but also create a sense of pride and trust in locally farmed products.

The expansion of domestic retail and distribution networks has further facilitated market growth for aquaculture products. Supermarkets, grocery stores, and online platforms now offer a wide variety of fresh and value-added seafood products, making them more accessible to consumers. The rise of e-commerce has been particularly transformative, allowing consumers to purchase seafood directly from producers or through specialized online marketplaces. This shift has not only enhanced convenience but also strengthened the connection between aquaculture farmers and local communities.

Small-scale and artisanal aquaculture operations play a significant role in meeting domestic market demand. In rural areas, these producers often supply local markets with affordable and fresh fish, contributing to food security and rural development. Additionally, community-based aquaculture projects have empowered smallholders and marginalized groups, enabling them to participate in domestic supply chains and improve their livelihoods. The integration of small-scale producers into formal markets enhances the diversity and resilience of domestic aquaculture industries.

Domestic market growth has also been bolstered by innovations in aquaculture production and processing. Advanced farming techniques, such as RAS and biofloc technology, have increased production efficiency and reduced costs, making aquaculture products more affordable for consumers. Similarly, value-added processing, including filleting, freezing, and ready-to-cook packaging, enhances the convenience and appeal of aquaculture products, further driving market demand.

Despite its growth, the domestic aquaculture market faces challenges that must be addressed to sustain its momentum. Price volatility, competition with imported seafood, and gaps in infrastructure and cold chain logistics can hinder market development. Strengthening these areas is essential to ensure that domestic aquaculture products remain competitive and accessible to consumers. Additionally, fostering consumer confidence through transparent labeling, quality assurance, and certification programs is critical for building trust in locally produced seafood.

The growth of domestic markets for aquaculture reflects the sector's ability to adapt to changing consumer preferences and socioeconomic conditions. By meeting local demand, creating economic opportunities, and reducing reliance on imports, domestic aquaculture markets contribute to national food security and economic resilience.

4.3. Social Challenges in Aquaculture Expansion

The expansion of aquaculture, while essential for meeting global food demands, presents significant social challenges, including resource access conflicts, community displacement, and equity issues, which must be addressed to ensure sustainable and inclusive growth.

4.3.1. Access to Resources and Equity Issues

The rapid expansion of aquaculture has brought to light significant challenges related to access to resources and equity, particularly in regions where competition for land, water, and coastal areas is intense. Ensuring that the benefits of aquaculture are equitably distributed while minimizing conflicts over resource use is critical for fostering sustainable and inclusive growth in the sector.

Access to land and water resources is a central issue in aquaculture development. Aquaculture farms, especially those located in coastal and inland areas, often require large tracts of land or access to water bodies, leading to competition with other land uses such as agriculture, tourism, and urban development. In many cases, small-scale fishers and farmers, who rely on these resources for their livelihoods, are disproportionately affected. Large-scale commercial aquaculture operations can displace traditional users, reducing their access to vital resources and exacerbating social inequalities.

Coastal aquaculture, particularly shrimp and fish farming, has been a source of conflict in many developing countries. Mangrove deforestation and the conversion of wetlands into aquaculture ponds have not only caused environmental degradation but also displaced local communities that depend on these ecosystems for fishing, farming, and gathering forest products. This loss of access to natural resources can lead to reduced income and food insecurity for marginalized populations, particularly indigenous groups and small-scale fishers who often lack legal recognition of their resource rights.

Equity issues in aquaculture are also evident in the distribution of economic benefits. While large-scale aquaculture operations generate significant revenue and employment opportunities, these benefits are not always shared equitably. Small-scale producers, who form the backbone of aquaculture in many regions, often face barriers to accessing markets, technology, and financing, limiting their ability to compete with industrial-scale farms. This creates a widening gap between large and small producers, further marginalizing vulnerable groups and perpetuating social inequalities.

The allocation of water resources for aquaculture also raises equity concerns, particularly in regions where water scarcity is a growing challenge. Aquaculture operations often require substantial volumes of freshwater for pond filling, irrigation, and water quality maintenance, which can strain local water supplies. In some cases, the prioritization of water use for aquaculture has reduced access for agricultural, domestic, and community needs, creating tensions between stakeholders. Women and marginalized groups, who are often responsible for managing household water resources, are disproportionately affected by these inequities.

Legal and institutional frameworks play a critical role in determining access to resources and equity in aquaculture. In many countries, weak governance and unclear property rights exacerbate conflicts over land and water use. Small-scale producers and local communities often lack the legal recognition or political influence needed to defend their resource rights against more powerful stakeholders. Strengthening legal protections and participatory governance mechanisms is essential for ensuring that resource allocation processes are transparent, inclusive, and equitable.

Efforts to address access and equity issues in aquaculture are gaining traction globally. Initiatives that promote the inclusion of small-scale producers, indigenous groups, and marginalized communities in decision-making processes are helping to create more equitable aquaculture systems. Community-based resource management, for example, empowers local stakeholders to participate in the planning and regulation of aquaculture activities, ensuring that their needs and priorities are considered.

The development of cooperatives and producer associations has also proven effective in enhancing equity in aquaculture. These organizations enable small-scale producers to pool resources, access financing, and negotiate better terms with buyers and regulators. By strengthening their collective bargaining power, cooperatives help level the playing field and ensure that smallholders can compete in increasingly globalized aquaculture markets.

Technology and innovation also have the potential to address resource access and equity challenges in aquaculture. Low-cost and scalable technologies, such as mobile apps for market access or affordable water management systems, can empower small-scale producers to improve productivity and efficiency. Capacity-building programs that provide training in sustainable practices and business management further enhance the ability of marginalized groups to participate in and benefit from aquaculture.

Addressing access to resources and equity issues is essential for ensuring the sustainability and inclusivity of aquaculture. By promoting fair resource allocation, strengthening legal protections, and empowering marginalized groups, the aquaculture sector can contribute to social cohesion and equitable economic development.

4.3.2. Community Resistance to Aquaculture Projects

Community resistance to aquaculture projects is a growing challenge that can significantly impact the expansion and success of the sector. While aquaculture offers opportunities for economic growth, food security, and employment, the perception of negative social and environmental consequences often leads to opposition from local communities. Understanding the causes of this resistance is crucial for addressing conflicts and ensuring that aquaculture projects are developed in a socially inclusive and sustainable manner.

One of the primary drivers of community resistance is the perceived environmental impact of aquaculture operations. Concerns about water pollution, habitat destruction, and biodiversity loss are commonly raised by communities living near aquaculture farms. Effluents from fish farms, including uneaten feed, feces, and chemicals, can degrade water quality and disrupt local ecosystems, leading to conflicts with communities that depend on these resources for fishing, farming, or domestic use. For example, in coastal areas, the destruction of mangroves to create shrimp ponds has displaced traditional users and raised concerns about the long-term sustainability of such practices.

Competition for resources is another significant factor fueling community resistance. Large-scale aquaculture projects often require extensive access to land and water, which can encroach on the resources traditionally used by local communities. In many cases, small-scale fishers, farmers, and indigenous groups are excluded from decision-making processes, leading to perceptions of inequity and marginalization. The privatization of coastal or freshwater resources for aquaculture can further exacerbate tensions, as local users may feel that their rights are being ignored or undermined.

Economic disparities and unequal benefit distribution also contribute to resistance. While aquaculture projects may generate significant revenue and create employment opportunities, these benefits are not always equitably shared with local communities. Large commercial operations often prioritize profits over local development, leaving communities to bear the social and environmental costs. For instance, jobs created by aquaculture projects may favor skilled workers from outside the community, while locals are left with low-paying or precarious positions. This inequity reinforces feelings of exclusion and fuels opposition.

Social and cultural factors also play a role in community resistance to aquaculture. Many communities have deep cultural and historical connections to their natural environments, which can be disrupted by large-scale aquaculture development. Changes to traditional practices, such as artisanal fishing or farming, may be seen as a threat to cultural identity and heritage. Furthermore, the influx of outside investors and workers into local areas can create social tensions, particularly if there is limited engagement with or understanding of the community's values and needs.

Health and safety concerns are another source of resistance. Communities living near aquaculture farms often express fears about the potential health risks associated with pollution, disease outbreaks, and the use of antibiotics or chemicals in farming operations. Misinformation or a lack of transparency regarding aquaculture practices can amplify these concerns, leading to heightened opposition.

Effective engagement and communication are critical for addressing community resistance to aquaculture projects. Transparent consultation processes that involve local stakeholders from the planning stages can help build trust and ensure that community concerns are considered. Collaborative approaches, such as participatory planning and decision-making, allow communities to voice their perspectives and contribute to project design, reducing opposition and fostering a sense of ownership.

Economic incentives and benefit-sharing mechanisms can also play a role in mitigating resistance. Ensuring that local communities receive tangible benefits from aquaculture projects, such as employment opportunities, infrastructure development, or community investment programs, can help address perceptions of inequity. Capacity-building initiatives that provide training and resources for local residents to participate in aquaculture can further enhance community support.

Environmental safeguards and sustainable practices are essential for minimizing the ecological impacts that drive community resistance. Adopting technologies and systems that reduce pollution, protect habitats, and enhance resource efficiency can demonstrate a commitment to sustainability and address community concerns. Certification programs, such as those offered by the ASC, provide transparency and assurance that projects adhere to environmental and social standards.

Community resistance to aquaculture projects underscores the importance of balancing economic development with social inclusion and environmental sustainability. By addressing the root causes of resistance and fostering meaningful collaboration with local communities, the aquaculture sector can navigate conflicts and contribute to equitable and sustainable growth.

Chapter 5. Innovations in Aquaculture for Food Security

Aquaculture is at the forefront of addressing global food security challenges, with innovations driving advancements in sustainability, efficiency, and productivity. From cutting-edge technologies to novel farming practices, these developments are reshaping the industry and its ability to meet growing food demands. This chapter explores the latest innovations in aquaculture, focusing on how they contribute to sustainable production, improve resource use, and enhance resilience in the face of environmental and social challenges.

5.1. Role of Biotechnology in Aquaculture

Biotechnology plays a transformative role in aquaculture, offering innovative solutions to enhance productivity, sustainability, and disease management while addressing the growing demand for high-quality aquatic products.

5.1.1. Genetic Improvement for Disease Resistance

Genetic improvement has emerged as a critical tool in aquaculture, addressing one of the industry's most persistent challenges: disease outbreaks. Diseases can devastate aquaculture operations, leading to significant economic losses, reduced production efficiency, and threats to food security. The application of genetic techniques to enhance disease resistance in farmed aquatic species offers a sustainable and effective solution, minimizing the reliance on antibiotics and chemicals while improving overall productivity.

Selective breeding is one of the most widely used approaches for genetic improvement in aquaculture. By identifying and breeding individuals with desirable traits, such as enhanced resistance to specific pathogens, producers can gradually improve the health and resilience of farmed populations. For example, selective breeding programs have been successfully implemented in Atlantic salmon (*Salmo salar*), where individuals resistant to sea lice and viral diseases like infectious pancreatic necrosis (IPN) are bred over successive generations. These programs not only reduce mortality rates but also decrease the need for chemical treatments, improving the environmental sustainability of aquaculture operations.

Another powerful genetic tool is marker-assisted selection (MAS), which combines traditional breeding methods with molecular biology. MAS involves identifying genetic markers linked to disease resistance and using these markers to select individuals for breeding. This approach accelerates the breeding process by enabling the early identification of resistant traits, even before disease exposure. For instance, MAS has been applied to tilapia (*Oreochromis niloticus*) to improve resistance to bacterial diseases like *Streptococcus* and *Aeromonas*, resulting in healthier stocks and higher production yields.

Gene editing technologies, particularly CRISPR-Cas9, are revolutionizing genetic improvement in aquaculture by enabling precise modifications of an organism's DNA. Gene editing can be used to directly enhance disease resistance by targeting and altering genes associated with immune responses or pathogen susceptibility. For example, researchers have used CRISPR-Cas9 to edit the genome of catfish, improving their resistance to viral infections and parasitic infestations. Unlike traditional selective breeding, gene editing offers a faster and more targeted approach, making it a promising tool for addressing emerging disease challenges in aquaculture.

Transgenic technology is another genetic improvement method with significant potential for enhancing disease resistance. This involves introducing specific genes from other organisms to confer resistance to particular pathogens. For instance, transgenic tilapia with enhanced resistance to bacterial infections have been developed by incorporating genes from other fish species. While transgenic approaches remain controversial due to regulatory and public acceptance issues, they offer a powerful solution for combating diseases in aquaculture systems where conventional methods fall short.

Improving disease resistance through genetic enhancement has far-reaching benefits for the aquaculture industry. Healthier stocks lead to higher survival rates, improved growth performance, and increased efficiency in feed conversion. These outcomes translate into economic gains for producers, as well as a more stable and reliable supply of seafood for consumers. Furthermore, reducing the reliance on antibiotics and chemicals contributes to environmental sustainability by minimizing the risk of antimicrobial resistance and pollution in aquatic ecosystems.

However, implementing genetic improvement programs for disease resistance is not without challenges. One major hurdle is the potential for reduced genetic diversity in farmed populations due to the selective breeding of specific traits. Reduced diversity can increase the vulnerability of stocks to other diseases or environmental stressors, potentially offsetting the benefits of genetic improvement. To address this, breeding programs must carefully manage genetic diversity and incorporate strategies to maintain a broad gene pool.

Ethical and regulatory considerations also play a role in the adoption of advanced genetic techniques such as gene editing and transgenics. Concerns about the safety, environmental impact, and consumer acceptance of genetically modified organisms (GMOs) can limit the application of these technologies in aquaculture. Transparent communication, robust regulatory frameworks, and public education are essential to address these concerns and build trust in the benefits of genetic improvement.

Capacity building and infrastructure development are critical for enabling the widespread adoption of genetic improvement technologies in aquaculture. Many small-scale and developing-country producers lack access to the resources and expertise needed to implement these programs. Investments in research, training, and technology transfer can help bridge this gap, ensuring that genetic improvement benefits a wide range of stakeholders and contributes to global food security.

Genetic improvement for disease resistance is transforming aquaculture by providing sustainable and innovative solutions to one of the industry's most pressing challenges. As technology continues to advance, the integration of these tools into aquaculture systems will play a vital role in enhancing resilience, productivity, and sustainability across the sector.

5.1.2. Enhancing Growth Rates in Aquatic Species

Enhancing growth rates in aquatic species is a key focus of biotechnology in aquaculture, as faster growth translates into shorter production cycles, increased yields, and improved economic viability. By applying genetic, molecular, and environmental techniques, researchers and producers are developing innovative solutions to optimize growth rates while maintaining the health and sustainability of farmed stocks.

Selective breeding has long been a foundational method for improving growth rates in aquaculture. This process involves identifying and breeding individuals that exhibit superior growth performance, resulting in successive generations with enhanced growth traits. For example, in tilapia (*Oreochromis niloticus*), selective breeding programs have achieved significant increases in growth rates, making tilapia one of the most widely farmed species globally. Similarly, Atlantic salmon (*Salmo salar*) and shrimp species such as Pacific white shrimp (*Litopenaeus vannamei*) have benefited from breeding programs that focus on size, weight gain, and feed conversion efficiency. These improvements not only reduce production costs but also increase market competitiveness for producers.

MAS is an advanced approach to enhancing growth rates, combining traditional breeding methods with molecular biology. By identifying genetic markers associated with growth-related traits, MAS enables more precise selection of individuals for breeding. This accelerates the process of developing fast-growing populations and reduces the risk of unintended negative traits. In species like catfish and carp, MAS has been used successfully to enhance growth rates while maintaining resilience to environmental stressors and diseases.

Gene editing technologies, such as CRISPR-Cas9, have opened new possibilities for directly enhancing growth rates in aquatic species. Gene editing allows scientists to modify specific genes responsible for growth regulation, metabolic processes, or feed efficiency. For example, researchers have used CRISPR-Cas9 to edit the genes of tilapia and salmon, targeting growth hormone pathways to improve growth rates without compromising the overall health of the fish. Gene editing provides a faster and more precise alternative to traditional breeding methods, offering significant potential for scaling up production.

Transgenic technology is another avenue for enhancing growth rates in aquaculture. Transgenic fish, such as genetically modified Atlantic salmon, have been developed by introducing growth hormone-regulating genes from other species. These salmon grow to market size in about half the time of their non-transgenic counterparts, significantly increasing productivity and reducing resource use. However, transgenic approaches face regulatory and public acceptance challenges, which limit their widespread application despite their demonstrated effectiveness.

Environmental and nutritional management also play critical roles in enhancing growth rates. Optimal water quality, temperature, and oxygen levels are essential for promoting healthy growth in aquatic species. Advances in RAS and real-time monitoring technologies have enabled producers to maintain precise control over environmental conditions, ensuring that farmed stocks grow under optimal conditions. Nutritional improvements, such as the development of high-performance feeds tailored to the specific needs of species, further support rapid and efficient growth. Feed formulations enriched with essential amino acids, vitamins, and minerals have been shown to improve feed conversion ratios and accelerate growth in species like shrimp, trout, and sea bass.

The integration of precision aquaculture techniques is further enhancing growth rates in aquaculture. Automated feeding systems, powered by AI and sensors, optimize feeding schedules and quantities based on real-time data on fish behavior and environmental parameters. These systems minimize feed waste, reduce costs, and maximize growth potential by ensuring that fish receive adequate nutrition without overfeeding. Precision aquaculture technologies are particularly valuable in large-scale operations, where efficiency and consistency are critical.

Enhancing growth rates in aquatic species has significant economic and environmental implications. Faster growth reduces the time to market, improving profitability for producers and ensuring a steady supply of seafood for consumers. Shorter production cycles also lower resource use, such as feed and water, contributing to the sustainability of aquaculture operations. By improving feed efficiency, faster-growing species generate less waste, reducing the environmental impact of farming activities.

Despite these benefits, challenges remain in the pursuit of enhanced growth rates. The risk of negative trade-offs, such as reduced disease resistance or compromised reproductive performance, must be carefully managed. Breeding and genetic modification programs need to balance growth traits with overall health and resilience to ensure the long-term viability of farmed stocks. Additionally, regulatory and ethical considerations surrounding gene editing and transgenic technologies require transparent frameworks to address public concerns and build trust in these innovations.

Capacity-building and knowledge-sharing initiatives are essential for enabling widespread adoption of growth-enhancing techniques in aquaculture. Many small-scale producers lack access to advanced technologies or training, limiting their ability to benefit from these innovations. Investments in research, education, and technology transfer can bridge this gap, ensuring that the advantages of enhanced growth rates are accessible to all stakeholders.

Enhancing growth rates in aquatic species represents a critical advancement in aquaculture, addressing the dual challenges of meeting global seafood demand and ensuring sustainable production. Through continued innovation and collaboration, biotechnology-driven growth improvements will play a pivotal role in shaping the future of aquaculture and global food systems.

5.2. Digitalization in Aquaculture

Digitalization is transforming aquaculture by introducing advanced technologies such as sensors, AI, and data analytics to optimize production, enhance sustainability, and improve decision-making across the sector.

5.2.1. Smart Aquaculture Monitoring Systems

Smart aquaculture monitoring systems are revolutionizing the aquaculture industry by integrating advanced technologies to enhance operational efficiency, sustainability, and productivity. These systems utilize a combination of sensors, data analytics, and automation to provide real-time insights into key parameters affecting the health and growth of aquatic species, as well as the overall performance of aquaculture operations.

At the heart of smart aquaculture systems are sensors designed to monitor a wide range of environmental and biological factors. These include water temperature, dissolved oxygen levels, pH, salinity, turbidity, and ammonia concentrations. By continuously collecting and transmitting data, these sensors enable farmers to maintain optimal conditions for their farmed species, reducing the risk of stress, disease, and mortality. For instance, maintaining stable dissolved oxygen levels is critical for fish health, and automated aeration systems linked to real-time oxygen sensors ensure that levels are adjusted as needed.

In addition to environmental monitoring, smart systems also track biological data, such as the growth rates, health status, and feeding behavior of farmed species. Underwater cameras and acoustic sensors are commonly used to observe fish behavior, allowing farmers to detect abnormalities that may indicate stress or disease. These technologies also help optimize feeding practices by analyzing fish movements and appetite, reducing feed waste and improving feed conversion efficiency.

Data analytics plays a crucial role in smart aquaculture monitoring systems, transforming raw data into actionable insights. Advanced algorithms and machine learning models process the data collected by sensors to identify patterns and predict potential issues. For example, predictive analytics can forecast the likelihood of disease outbreaks based on water quality trends or environmental changes, enabling farmers to take preventive measures. Similarly, growth models help optimize harvesting schedules, ensuring that fish reach market size efficiently while maintaining high-quality standards.

Automation is another key component of smart aquaculture systems, enabling precise and timely responses to changing conditions. Automated feeders, for instance, dispense feed based on data from sensors and cameras, ensuring that fish are fed the right amount at the right time. Similarly, water treatment systems automatically adjust pH, salinity, or oxygen levels to maintain ideal conditions. These automated responses not only improve productivity but also reduce labor costs and minimize human error.

The integration of smart aquaculture systems with remote monitoring capabilities has further enhanced their utility. Cloud-based platforms allow farmers to access real-time data and control their operations from anywhere using smartphones or computers. This remote access is particularly valuable for large-scale or offshore aquaculture operations, where on-site monitoring may be challenging. By providing continuous oversight, remote monitoring systems help ensure the stability and resilience of aquaculture operations.

Smart aquaculture monitoring systems also contribute to sustainability by improving resource efficiency and minimizing environmental impacts. By optimizing feed usage, these systems reduce nutrient pollution and the associated risks of eutrophication in aquatic ecosystems. Real-time monitoring of water quality ensures that effluents are managed effectively, protecting surrounding environments. Additionally, the ability to predict and prevent disease outbreaks reduces the need for antibiotics and other chemicals, supporting healthier ecosystems and aligning with consumer demands for sustainable seafood.

Despite their advantages, the adoption of smart aquaculture monitoring systems faces challenges, particularly for small-scale and developing-country producers. The high upfront costs of sensors, data analytics software, and automation equipment can be a barrier to entry. Furthermore, the effective use of these systems requires technical expertise and training, which may not be readily available to all producers. Addressing these challenges requires investment in affordable technologies, capacity-building initiatives, and partnerships to support small-scale farmers in adopting smart systems.

The role of smart aquaculture monitoring systems is expected to expand as technology continues to advance. Innovations such as the Internet of Things (IoT), AI, and blockchain are being integrated into aquaculture systems, further enhancing their capabilities. IoT devices enable seamless communication between sensors, equipment, and cloud platforms, creating interconnected systems that optimize aquaculture operations in real time. AI algorithms improve predictive analytics and decision-making, while blockchain enhances traceability and transparency, building trust in the aquaculture supply chain.

Smart aquaculture monitoring systems represent a transformative approach to aquaculture, leveraging technology to address the challenges of productivity, sustainability, and resource efficiency. By providing real-time insights and enabling data-driven decision-making, these systems empower farmers to optimize their operations and meet the growing demand for sustainable seafood. As adoption expands, smart monitoring systems will play an increasingly critical role in shaping the future of aquaculture.

5.2.2. Big Data and Artificial Intelligence in Aquaculture

Big data and AI are transforming aquaculture by enabling precise, data-driven decision-making and improving the efficiency, sustainability, and productivity of farming operations. As the aquaculture industry grows to meet increasing global seafood demand, the ability to analyze vast amounts of data and predict outcomes with AI is revolutionizing traditional practices and paving the way for smarter, more resilient systems.

Big data in aquaculture refers to the collection and processing of extensive datasets generated from sensors, cameras, and other monitoring devices used in farming operations. These data streams capture critical information on environmental parameters such as water temperature, dissolved oxygen, salinity, and pH, as well as biological metrics such as fish growth rates, feeding behavior, and health status. The ability to store and analyze this data in real time allows farmers to monitor trends, identify anomalies, and optimize operations for improved outcomes.

AI takes big data analysis a step further by applying advanced algorithms and machine learning models to uncover patterns, predict future scenarios, and automate complex decision-making processes. For instance, AI-driven models can analyze historical water quality data to forecast environmental changes, enabling farmers to take preventive measures against conditions that could lead to stress or disease in farmed species. Similarly, growth prediction algorithms use data on fish size, feeding history, and water quality to estimate the optimal harvesting time, maximizing yields and market value.

One of the most significant applications of big data and AI in aquaculture is in precision feeding. Feeding represents one of the largest costs in aquaculture operations, and overfeeding can lead to wasted resources and nutrient pollution in aquatic environments. AI-powered feeding systems analyze real-time data from underwater cameras and acoustic sensors to assess fish appetite and behavior. Based on this analysis, these systems determine the exact amount of feed required, reducing waste, improving feed conversion ratios, and lowering costs. This approach not only enhances profitability but also minimizes the environmental footprint of aquaculture operations.

Disease management is another area where big data and AI are making a substantial impact. Early detection and prevention of diseases are critical for maintaining healthy stocks and minimizing economic losses. AI models trained on large datasets of disease indicators, such as fish behavior, water quality changes, and historical outbreaks, can identify early warning signs of disease outbreaks. These systems provide actionable insights, allowing farmers to implement targeted interventions such as adjusting water quality, modifying stocking densities, or applying treatments. This proactive approach reduces dependency on antibiotics and supports sustainable aquaculture practices.

AI-driven predictive analytics also play a key role in optimizing site selection and farm management. By analyzing geospatial data, oceanographic conditions, and historical production data, AI systems can identify the most suitable locations for aquaculture operations. These insights help farmers choose sites with favorable environmental conditions, minimizing risks associated with extreme weather events, pollution, or unsuitable habitats. Additionally, big data analysis of farm operations enables benchmarking and continuous improvement, helping producers identify best practices and enhance overall efficiency.

Blockchain technology, when integrated with big data and AI, enhances traceability and transparency in the aquaculture supply chain. By recording and verifying every stage of production, from hatchery to harvest to market, blockchain systems ensure that consumers and retailers can access detailed information about the origin and sustainability of aquaculture products. AI algorithms analyze this supply chain data to optimize logistics, reduce waste, and improve the traceability of seafood products, aligning with consumer demand for sustainable and ethical sourcing.

While the integration of big data and AI offers immense benefits, its adoption comes with challenges. One major barrier is the cost of implementing advanced technologies, including sensors, data storage systems, and AI software. Small-scale producers, in particular, may struggle to afford these investments, creating a digital divide within the industry. Additionally, the effective use of AI requires access to high-quality data and skilled personnel to develop and maintain AI models. Ensuring data accuracy, consistency, and interoperability is critical for achieving reliable and actionable insights.

Another challenge is the ethical use of AI in aquaculture. Concerns about data privacy, algorithmic bias, and the displacement of traditional knowledge must be addressed to ensure that technological advancements benefit all stakeholders equitably. Collaborative efforts among industry players, governments, and research institutions are essential for developing guidelines and standards that promote responsible and inclusive use of AI in aquaculture.

Despite these challenges, the future of big data and AI in aquaculture is promising. Continued advancements in machine learning, IoT devices, and cloud computing are expected to make these technologies more accessible and cost-effective. Partnerships between technology providers and aquaculture producers will further drive innovation and adoption, enabling the industry to harness the full potential of big data and AI.

Big data and AI are reshaping aquaculture by unlocking new possibilities for precision farming, sustainability, and profitability. By leveraging these technologies, the industry can address pressing challenges, optimize resource use, and ensure the production of high-quality seafood to meet global demand. As adoption expands, big data and AI will become indispensable tools for driving the future of aquaculture.

5.3. Circular Economy Principles in Aquaculture

Circular economy principles in aquaculture aim to transform the industry by maximizing resource efficiency, minimizing waste, and creating sustainable systems that align with environmental and economic goals.

5.3.1. Recycling Nutrients and By-products

Recycling nutrients and by-products in aquaculture is a cornerstone of circular economy principles, transforming what was traditionally considered waste into valuable resources. By reusing and repurposing materials within aquaculture systems, producers can enhance sustainability, reduce environmental impacts, and improve economic efficiency. This approach addresses critical challenges such as nutrient pollution, resource depletion, and waste management while fostering innovation and resilience in the industry.

One of the primary sources of waste in aquaculture is nutrient-rich effluents, which include uneaten feed, fish feces, and dissolved organic compounds. When discharged into the environment, these effluents can cause nutrient pollution, leading to eutrophication and degradation of aquatic ecosystems. Recycling these nutrients within aquaculture systems not only mitigates environmental harm but also provides opportunities to enhance productivity. IMTA is a leading example of this practice, where nutrient-rich waste from fish or shrimp farming serves as a resource for other species. Seaweed and bivalves, for instance, absorb dissolved nutrients, converting them into biomass that can be harvested and utilized for food, feed, or biofuels. This closed-loop system reduces nutrient loss while creating additional revenue streams for farmers.

Solid waste, such as fish feces and uneaten feed, can also be collected and repurposed through innovative waste management practices. Technologies like sedimentation systems and biofloc technology capture solid waste, which can then be processed into organic fertilizers or soil amendments. These by-products are rich in nutrients like nitrogen, phosphorus, and potassium, making them valuable for agricultural use. By recycling solid waste into fertilizers, aquaculture not only reduces its environmental footprint but also contributes to sustainable farming practices on land.

The use of aquaculture by-products in animal feed is another promising avenue for nutrient recycling. Fish processing generates significant amounts of waste, including heads, bones, and viscera, which traditionally go unused or are discarded. These by-products can be processed into fishmeal and fish oil, essential components of aquaculture feed for carnivorous species like salmon and trout. Advances in processing technology, such as enzymatic hydrolysis, have improved the quality and digestibility of by-product-derived feed ingredients, enhancing their value and reducing dependence on wild-caught fish for feed production.

Microbial technologies are also playing a significant role in nutrient recycling. Anaerobic digestion systems convert organic waste from aquaculture into biogas, a renewable energy source, and nutrient-rich digestate, which can be used as fertilizer. This dual benefit of energy production and nutrient recovery aligns with circular economy goals, creating synergies between aquaculture and renewable energy systems. Similarly, biofilters and microbial consortia are used in RAS to break down waste products, maintaining water quality while recovering nutrients for reuse.

Recycling nutrients and by-products extends beyond aquaculture operations to broader industrial applications. Seaweed farming, for example, utilizes excess nutrients from aquaculture effluents to grow biomass that can be processed into bioplastics, pharmaceuticals, and cosmetics. These high-value products provide additional economic incentives for nutrient recycling while contributing to sustainable industrial practices. Similarly, shrimp shells and other crustacean by-products are rich in chitin, a versatile biopolymer used in medical, agricultural, and environmental applications. Extracting chitin and its derivatives from aquaculture by-products adds value to waste streams and reduces material waste.

Collaboration between aquaculture and other sectors is crucial for maximizing the benefits of nutrient recycling. Partnerships with agriculture, energy, and manufacturing industries create opportunities for resource sharing and innovation. For instance, integrated aquaponics systems combine fish farming with hydroponic vegetable cultivation, where nutrient-rich effluents from aquaculture serve as fertilizers for plants. This closed-loop system not only recycles nutrients but also diversifies production, improving food security and economic resilience.

Despite its potential, scaling up nutrient recycling in aquaculture faces several challenges. The cost of implementing advanced waste management technologies can be prohibitive for small-scale producers, particularly in developing regions. Regulatory barriers and a lack of standardization in by-product utilization further hinder the widespread adoption of nutrient recycling practices. Investments in research, infrastructure, and policy development are essential to overcome these barriers and create enabling environments for circular economy practices in aquaculture.

Public awareness and consumer acceptance also play a role in the success of nutrient recycling initiatives. Educating consumers about the environmental benefits and safety of products derived from recycled nutrients can drive demand and support market growth. Certification schemes and labeling programs that highlight sustainable practices in aquaculture further build trust and incentivize producers to adopt nutrient recycling technologies.

Recycling nutrients and by-products is a transformative approach that integrates sustainability into every stage of aquaculture production. By closing resource loops, reducing waste, and creating value from by-products, nutrient recycling contributes to a more sustainable, efficient, and resilient aquaculture industry. As technologies and practices continue to evolve, nutrient recycling will remain central to achieving circular economy goals and addressing the environmental and economic challenges of modern aquaculture.

5.3.2. Zero-Waste Aquaculture Systems

Zero-waste aquaculture systems represent a paradigm shift in sustainable aquaculture, aiming to eliminate waste generation by optimizing resource use and recycling by-products. By integrating innovative technologies and practices, these systems transform conventional aquaculture into closed-loop operations that minimize environmental impacts while maximizing productivity. Zero-waste aquaculture aligns with circular economy principles, creating systems that are not only efficient but also economically and environmentally sustainable.

At the core of zero-waste aquaculture systems is the concept of resource cycling, where waste products from one stage of production serve as inputs for another. IMTA is a prime example of this approach. In IMTA systems, nutrient-rich effluents from fish or shrimp farming are absorbed by filter feeders like mussels and oysters, and further utilized by seaweed, which takes up dissolved nutrients. This integration reduces nutrient pollution, enhances water quality, and produces multiple outputs, such as seafood and seaweed-based products, within a single system. The circular nature of IMTA allows for near-complete utilization of resources, significantly reducing waste.

RAS are another cornerstone of zero-waste aquaculture. RAS operates in a closed-loop environment, where water is continuously filtered and reused, minimizing water consumption and effluent discharge. Mechanical and biological filtration systems in RAS remove solid and dissolved waste, which can be further processed into valuable by-products such as fertilizers or biogas. This water-efficient design not only addresses water scarcity challenges but also prevents nutrient-rich effluents from polluting natural ecosystems.

Solid waste, such as uneaten feed and fish feces, is a significant concern in conventional aquaculture systems. Zero-waste aquaculture addresses this challenge by capturing and repurposing these materials. Technologies like sedimentation tanks and waste

76

traps collect solid waste, which can then be converted into organic fertilizers or soil conditioners through composting or anaerobic digestion. The resulting products contribute to sustainable agriculture, creating synergies between aquaculture and farming industries.

Biofloc technology is an innovative zero-waste approach widely adopted in shrimp and tilapia farming. In biofloc systems, microbial communities break down organic waste within the culture water, converting it into protein-rich biomass that serves as an additional feed source for farmed species. This self-sustaining system not only reduces external feed requirements but also prevents waste accumulation, ensuring a balanced and healthy aquatic environment.

Zero-waste aquaculture systems also extend to the processing and post-harvest stages. The seafood processing industry generates significant quantities of by-products, including fish heads, bones, and viscera. In a zero-waste framework, these by-products are utilized to produce fishmeal, fish oil, collagen, and other value-added products. Advanced processing technologies, such as enzymatic hydrolysis, improve the efficiency and quality of by-product utilization, ensuring that no part of the fish goes to waste. For example, fish skins can be processed into gelatin for the food industry, while fish scales can be used to extract collagen for cosmetic and pharmaceutical applications.

The integration of renewable energy technologies further enhances the sustainability of zero-waste aquaculture systems. Waste-to-energy solutions, such as anaerobic digestion, convert organic waste into biogas, providing a renewable source of energy for on-site operations. Solar panels and wind turbines can complement these systems, reducing reliance on fossil fuels and lowering the carbon footprint of aquaculture farms. By addressing both waste and energy challenges, these innovations contribute to the broader sustainability goals of the industry.

Automation and digitalization play a key role in the implementation of zero-waste aquaculture systems. Real-time monitoring and data analytics enable precise control over feeding, water quality, and waste management, minimizing resource wastage and optimizing system performance. For instance, automated feeding systems use sensors and AI algorithms to adjust feed delivery based on fish behavior, ensuring that feed is consumed efficiently without generating excess waste. Similarly, smart waste collection systems monitor and manage waste streams in real time, ensuring timely processing and recycling.

Collaboration between aquaculture and other sectors is essential for achieving zero-waste goals. Partnerships with agriculture, energy, and bioplastics industries open new avenues for resource sharing and by-product utilization. For example, seaweed cultivated in IMTA systems can be processed into biodegradable packaging materials, reducing plastic waste in the seafood supply chain. Similarly, nutrient-rich effluents from aquaculture can be used in hydroponic systems to grow vegetables, creating integrated systems that maximize resource efficiency.

Despite its benefits, transitioning to zero-waste aquaculture systems presents challenges. High initial costs, technical complexity, and the need for specialized expertise can deter producers, particularly small-scale farmers, from adopting these systems. Addressing these barriers requires investments in research, subsidies, and capacity-building programs to make zero-waste technologies accessible and economically viable for all stakeholders.

Regulatory frameworks and market incentives are also critical for promoting zero-waste aquaculture. Policies that encourage waste reduction, resource recycling, and sustainable practices can drive industry-wide adoption of zero-waste principles. Certification schemes and eco-labels that highlight zero-waste practices can enhance consumer trust and create market demand for sustainably produced aquaculture products.

Zero-waste aquaculture systems represent a transformative approach to sustainable food production, offering solutions to the environmental and resource challenges faced by the industry. By embracing innovative technologies, integrating circular economy principles, and fostering collaboration across sectors, aquaculture can evolve into a model of efficiency and sustainability. These systems not only minimize waste but also create new opportunities for economic growth and environmental stewardship, shaping the future of the global aquaculture industry.

Chapter 6. Policy and Governance for Sustainable Aquaculture

Effective policy and governance are crucial for ensuring the sustainable development of aquaculture. As the industry grows to meet global food demands, robust frameworks are needed to address environmental, social, and economic challenges. This chapter explores the role of policy and governance in regulating aquaculture practices, promoting sustainability, and balancing the interests of stakeholders, from small-scale farmers to large-scale producers and local communities. Through innovative strategies and international cooperation, governance can guide aquaculture toward a more resilient and equitable future.

6.1. National Policies for Aquaculture Development

National policies for aquaculture development play a pivotal role in shaping the industry's growth by establishing regulations, incentives, and frameworks that promote sustainable practices and address sector-specific challenges.

6.1.1. Regulatory Frameworks and Licensing

Regulatory frameworks and licensing systems form the backbone of national aquaculture governance, ensuring that industry growth is balanced with environmental protection, social equity, and economic sustainability. These frameworks provide the legal and institutional structures necessary to regulate aquaculture operations, allocate resources, and mitigate potential conflicts among stakeholders. Effective regulatory frameworks and licensing systems are essential for fostering a sustainable and well-managed aquaculture sector.

Licensing is a key component of regulatory frameworks, granting producers legal permission to establish and operate aquaculture facilities. Licensing systems typically outline the terms and conditions under which aquaculture activities can be conducted, including site selection, species cultivated, production methods, and environmental management practices. By enforcing these conditions, licensing authorities ensure that aquaculture operations comply with national laws and policies, reducing risks to ecosystems and communities.

Site selection is a critical aspect of the licensing process, as the location of aquaculture farms significantly influences their environmental and social impacts. Regulatory frameworks often require thorough environmental impact assessments (EIAs) as part of the licensing process to evaluate the suitability of proposed sites. These assessments consider factors such as water quality, biodiversity, and the potential for conflicts with other resource users, such as fisheries or tourism. By prioritizing sustainable site selection, licensing authorities help minimize habitat degradation, pollution, and resource competition.

Environmental regulations are central to licensing frameworks, addressing issues such as water use, effluent discharge, and waste management. Producers are often required to implement measures to prevent nutrient pollution, reduce waste, and maintain water quality in surrounding ecosystems. For example, regulations may mandate the use of RAS or IMTA to minimize environmental impacts. Compliance with these standards is monitored through periodic inspections and reporting requirements, ensuring accountability and continuous improvement.

Aquaculture licensing frameworks also address biosecurity, an essential aspect of sustainable aquaculture. Regulations often require producers to implement biosecurity measures to prevent the spread of diseases and invasive species. This includes protocols for stocking densities, quarantine procedures, and the use of certified disease-free fingerlings or juveniles. By enforcing biosecurity standards, licensing systems help protect both farmed and wild aquatic populations from disease outbreaks and genetic contamination.

Social considerations are increasingly integrated into regulatory frameworks and licensing processes. Many frameworks include provisions to safeguard the rights of local communities and small-scale producers, ensuring that aquaculture development does not lead to displacement or resource conflicts. For example, licensing systems may require stakeholder consultations and community engagement as part of the application process. These measures promote transparency, inclusivity, and equitable resource allocation, fostering social cohesion and local support for aquaculture projects.

Economic aspects of licensing frameworks focus on promoting investment and innovation while ensuring fair competition. Licensing systems may offer incentives, such as subsidies or tax breaks, to encourage sustainable practices and support small-scale or emerging producers. At the same time, regulations are designed to prevent monopolization and ensure that access to aquaculture opportunities is equitably distributed. Balancing these economic considerations is crucial for creating a dynamic and inclusive aquaculture sector.

Challenges in implementing regulatory frameworks and licensing systems often arise from capacity constraints, particularly in developing countries. Limited resources for monitoring and enforcement can lead to non-compliance, environmental degradation, and social conflicts. Addressing these challenges requires investment in capacity-building, technology, and infrastructure to strengthen regulatory institutions and improve the efficiency of licensing processes.

Harmonization of regulatory frameworks across regions is also important for addressing transboundary issues in aquaculture, such as shared water resources and international trade. Regional agreements and cooperation can help align standards and practices, promoting sustainable development and reducing conflicts. For example, regional bodies may establish guidelines for aquaculture licensing that consider ecological and economic contexts shared by neighboring countries.

Regulatory frameworks and licensing systems play a critical role in shaping the sustainable development of aquaculture. By balancing environmental, social, and economic considerations, these frameworks provide the foundation for a resilient and responsible industry. As the sector continues to evolve, adaptive and inclusive regulatory approaches will be essential for meeting emerging challenges and ensuring the long-term sustainability of aquaculture.

6.1.2. Incentives for Sustainable Practices

Incentives for sustainable practices in aquaculture are essential for encouraging producers to adopt environmentally responsible methods while ensuring economic viability. Governments and institutions worldwide have recognized the importance of aligning financial and regulatory incentives with sustainability goals to promote the long-term growth of the aquaculture sector. These incentives target various aspects of aquaculture operations, from reducing environmental impacts to enhancing social and economic outcomes, fostering a more resilient and sustainable industry.

Financial incentives, such as subsidies and grants, are among the most common tools used to promote sustainable practices in aquaculture. These programs provide direct support to producers who implement eco-friendly technologies and practices, such as RAS, biofloc technology, or IMTA. For example, subsidies may offset the high initial costs of installing water treatment systems, renewable energy sources, or waste management infrastructure. By reducing financial barriers, these incentives make sustainable practices more accessible, particularly for small-scale farmers and emerging producers.

Tax incentives are another effective mechanism to encourage sustainability in aquaculture. Governments may offer tax reductions or exemptions to producers who comply with environmental standards or invest in green technologies. For instance, tax breaks on the purchase of energy-efficient equipment or biodegradable materials can drive the adoption of sustainable production methods.

These incentives not only reduce operational costs but also create a competitive advantage for producers committed to sustainability.

Certification programs and eco-labels also act as powerful incentives for sustainable aquaculture practices. While not direct financial support, these programs provide market-based benefits by enabling producers to access premium markets and attract environmentally conscious consumers. Certification schemes, such as those provided by the ASC or Global GAP, require producers to meet stringent sustainability criteria related to water quality, feed efficiency, and social responsibility. Producers who achieve certification often benefit from higher product prices, increased demand, and improved market reputation, creating a strong incentive to adopt sustainable practices.

Loan programs and credit facilities designed specifically for sustainable aquaculture further incentivize eco-friendly operations. These financial tools offer favorable terms, such as low-interest rates or extended repayment periods, for projects that incorporate sustainability measures. For example, loans may be available for the development of offshore aquaculture systems that reduce pressure on coastal ecosystems or for the construction of hatcheries using renewable energy. By providing access to affordable capital, these programs empower producers to transition toward more sustainable practices.

Training and technical assistance programs also serve as indirect incentives by equipping producers with the knowledge and skills needed to implement sustainable methods. Workshops, extension services, and capacity-building initiatives help farmers understand the benefits of adopting eco-friendly technologies and practices. These programs often include demonstrations of cost-effective solutions, such as nutrient recycling systems or alternative feed sources, making sustainability more achievable for producers of all scales.

Public-private partnerships (PPPs) are increasingly being leveraged to create innovative incentive structures for sustainable aquaculture. Collaborations between governments, industry stakeholders, and non-governmental organizations (NGOs) combine financial support with technical expertise to promote sustainable practices. For instance, PPPs may fund research and development projects that focus on improving feed efficiency, reducing disease risks, or enhancing water quality. The results of these partnerships often lead to practical solutions that benefit the entire aquaculture industry.

Regulatory incentives also play a critical role in promoting sustainability. Governments may offer streamlined licensing processes or reduced fees for producers who meet or exceed environmental standards. These measures reward compliance and encourage producers to go beyond the minimum regulatory requirements. Similarly, recognition programs, such as sustainability awards or public commendations, highlight and reward exemplary practices, inspiring other producers to follow suit.

Despite their benefits, implementing effective incentive programs for sustainable aquaculture faces challenges. Financial constraints, limited awareness, and administrative inefficiencies can hinder the accessibility and impact of these programs, particularly for small-scale producers. Addressing these challenges requires targeted outreach, simplified application processes, and increased collaboration between stakeholders to ensure that incentives reach those who need them most.

Incentives for sustainable practices are a vital component of national policies for aquaculture development. By aligning economic support with environmental and social goals, these programs drive innovation and foster a culture of sustainability within the industry. As aquaculture continues to expand, well-designed incentive structures will play a crucial role in ensuring its long-term resilience and success.

6.2. International Cooperation in Aquaculture Governance

International cooperation in aquaculture governance is essential for addressing transboundary challenges, promoting sustainable practices, and ensuring the equitable development of the global aquaculture industry.

6.2.1. Role of Regional Agreements and Organizations

Regional agreements and organizations play a pivotal role in promoting sustainable aquaculture governance by fostering cooperation among countries to address shared challenges, harmonize regulations, and advance best practices. These entities provide a platform for collaboration, enabling nations to align their policies, pool resources, and collectively tackle issues such as environmental protection, resource management, and trade in aquaculture products. Through coordinated efforts, regional agreements and organizations contribute to the development of a resilient and sustainable aquaculture industry.

One of the primary functions of regional agreements is to establish common frameworks for aquaculture governance. These agreements outline shared goals and principles, such as ensuring food security, reducing environmental impacts, and supporting equitable access to resources. By adopting uniform standards, member countries can streamline regulatory processes, improve compliance, and facilitate cross-border trade. For example, the European Union (EU) has developed comprehensive aquaculture regulations under the Common Fisheries Policy (CFP), which provide guidelines for sustainable development, licensing, and environmental monitoring across member states.

Regional organizations also play a critical role in coordinating research and knowledge exchange among member countries. By facilitating joint studies and data sharing, these organizations help address knowledge gaps and promote innovation in aquaculture practices. For instance, the Network of Aquaculture Centres in Asia-Pacific (NACA) brings together governments, research institutions, and industry stakeholders to share expertise and develop region-specific solutions for sustainable aquaculture. NACA's initiatives focus on areas such as disease management, genetic improvement, and capacity building, benefiting producers and policymakers alike.

Transboundary resource management is another key area where regional agreements and organizations are indispensable. Many aquaculture systems rely on shared water resources, such as rivers, lakes, and coastal areas, which require cooperative management to prevent conflicts and ensure sustainability. Regional agreements often establish mechanisms for joint planning, monitoring, and enforcement to address issues like water quality, habitat conservation, and disease control. The Lake Victoria Fisheries Organization (LVFO), for example, oversees aquaculture development in the Lake Victoria Basin, promoting sustainable practices and mitigating the impacts of overfishing and pollution.

Harmonization of certification and trade standards is a significant focus of regional cooperation in aquaculture. Divergent regulations and certification requirements can create barriers to trade, particularly for small-scale producers. Regional organizations work to align standards for product quality, food safety, and environmental sustainability, enabling producers to access broader markets. The Association of Southeast Asian Nations (ASEAN), through its Guidelines on Responsible Fisheries and Aquaculture, provides a framework for harmonizing standards across member states, enhancing regional trade and competitiveness.

Regional agreements and organizations also facilitate capacity building and technical assistance, particularly in developing countries. Many small-scale producers face challenges such as limited access to technology, finance, and training. Regional initiatives provide resources and support to address these gaps, empowering producers to adopt sustainable practices and improve their livelihoods. For instance, the Southern African Development Community (SADC) implements aquaculture development programs that offer technical training, financial assistance, and market access support to member states.

Conflict resolution and dispute management are additional roles fulfilled by regional organizations. Transboundary issues, such as competition for water resources or the spread of aquatic diseases, can lead to tensions among neighboring countries. Regional agreements often include provisions for mediation and dispute resolution, ensuring that conflicts are addressed collaboratively and equitably. By fostering dialogue and mutual understanding, regional organizations contribute to the stability and cohesion of aquaculture governance.

Despite their contributions, regional agreements and organizations face challenges in achieving their goals. Limited funding, capacity constraints, and political differences among member countries can hinder the effectiveness of regional initiatives. Additionally, the diversity of aquaculture systems and practices across regions makes it difficult to develop universally applicable policies and standards. Addressing these challenges requires sustained investment, inclusive participation, and adaptive approaches that consider the unique needs and contexts of member countries.

The role of regional agreements and organizations in aquaculture governance is indispensable for addressing the complex and interconnected challenges facing the industry. By promoting cooperation, harmonization, and capacity building, these entities enable countries to work together toward a sustainable and equitable future for aquaculture. As the industry continues to grow, the importance of regional cooperation will only increase, making these agreements and organizations critical pillars of global aquaculture governance.

6.2.2. Addressing Transboundary Challenges in Aquaculture

Transboundary challenges in aquaculture arise from the shared nature of aquatic ecosystems and the interconnectedness of global trade and environmental impacts. These challenges include the spread of aquatic diseases, pollution of shared water resources, competition for marine and freshwater habitats, and the management of migratory species. Addressing these issues requires coordinated international efforts, supported by robust frameworks and cross-border collaboration to ensure sustainable aquaculture development.

One of the most pressing transboundary challenges in aquaculture is the spread of aquatic diseases. Pathogens and parasites can travel across borders through water systems, trade in live species, or the movement of contaminated equipment. Diseases such as infectious salmon anemia (ISA) and white spot syndrome in shrimp have caused significant economic losses and environmental harm. To address this, international cooperation focuses on harmonized biosecurity measures, disease monitoring, and rapid response systems. Organizations such as the World Organisation for Animal Health (OIE) develop guidelines for disease prevention and control, helping countries establish standardized practices to mitigate the spread of pathogens.

Pollution from aquaculture operations is another transboundary issue that affects shared water bodies, such as rivers, lakes, and coastal areas. Nutrient enrichment, chemical runoff, and organic waste from farms can lead to eutrophication and habitat degradation, impacting ecosystems and communities beyond national borders. Addressing this challenge requires joint efforts to regulate effluent discharge, promote sustainable farming practices, and restore affected ecosystems. For example, regional agreements like the Helsinki Commission (HELCOM) in the Baltic Sea region establish guidelines for reducing pollution from aquaculture and encourage member countries to collaborate on water quality monitoring and improvement programs.

Competition for shared resources, including water, land, and coastal areas, is a significant transboundary challenge. The expansion of aquaculture often conflicts with other uses of these resources, such as fisheries, agriculture, and tourism. In many cases, these conflicts exacerbate existing tensions between countries or regions.

Coordinated spatial planning and resource management frameworks can help balance competing interests and prevent disputes. Transboundary initiatives, such as the Nile Basin Initiative, bring together riparian states to develop equitable and sustainable strategies for aquaculture and other water-based activities.

The management of migratory species and shared fish stocks is another critical area of transboundary collaboration. Aquaculture operations can impact the health and populations of wild species that migrate across national boundaries. Escaped farmed fish, for instance, may interbreed with wild populations, affecting their genetic diversity and resilience. Coordinated efforts to regulate escape prevention measures, monitor migratory patterns, and protect wild stocks are essential for minimizing these impacts. Regional fisheries management organizations (RFMOs) often play a key role in addressing these challenges, ensuring that aquaculture development aligns with the conservation of shared marine resources.

Trade in aquaculture products also presents transboundary challenges, particularly concerning food safety, quality standards, and certification. Differences in regulations and standards between exporting and importing countries can create trade barriers and complicate market access. International organizations like the Food and Agriculture Organization (FAO) and the World Trade Organization (WTO) work to harmonize standards and facilitate fair trade practices. By addressing these disparities, countries can enhance the sustainability and competitiveness of the global aquaculture market.

Climate change further compounds transboundary challenges in aquaculture, as rising temperatures, changing ocean conditions, and extreme weather events affect ecosystems and aquaculture operations across borders. Collaborative research and data sharing are essential for understanding the impacts of climate change on aquaculture and developing adaptive strategies. Regional climate adaptation programs, such as those coordinated by the Coral Triangle Initiative, support countries in building resilience to climate-related challenges through joint planning and capacity building.

Despite the importance of international cooperation, addressing transboundary challenges in aquaculture faces significant obstacles. Political differences, resource constraints, and inadequate enforcement mechanisms can hinder collaborative efforts. Building trust among stakeholders, fostering inclusive participation, and ensuring equitable resource distribution are critical for overcoming these barriers.

Addressing transboundary challenges in aquaculture requires a comprehensive approach that combines technical expertise, policy coordination, and stakeholder engagement. By working together, countries and organizations can mitigate the risks associated with shared aquatic ecosystems and promote a sustainable future for global aquaculture. Through effective collaboration, transboundary challenges can become opportunities for innovation, cooperation, and shared progress.

6.3. Integrating Aquaculture into Food Security Policies

Integrating aquaculture into food security policies is essential for leveraging its potential to enhance global nutrition, support livelihoods, and address the growing demand for sustainable protein sources.

6.3.1. Aligning Aquaculture with National Food Strategies

Aligning aquaculture with national food strategies is a critical step in leveraging its potential to address food security challenges, improve nutrition, and support sustainable development. As global demand for protein continues to rise and natural resources face increasing pressures, integrating aquaculture into broader food strategies enables countries to maximize the sector's contributions to meeting dietary needs and ensuring equitable access to nutritious food.

A key aspect of aligning aquaculture with food strategies is recognizing its role as a reliable and scalable source of high-quality protein. Fish and other aquatic products are nutrient-dense foods, rich in essential fatty acids, vitamins, and minerals. National food strategies often aim to enhance dietary diversity and reduce malnutrition, particularly in vulnerable populations. Including aquaculture as a central component of these strategies ensures that its nutritional benefits are fully utilized. For example, integrating farmed fish into school meal programs or public health initiatives can help address deficiencies in omega-3 fatty acids and micronutrients in both urban and rural populations.

Policy alignment also involves promoting the accessibility and affordability of aquaculture products for domestic markets. While aquaculture is a major contributor to global seafood trade, much of the production in many countries is export-oriented, limiting local availability. National food strategies that prioritize local consumption of farmed aquatic products can improve food security and reduce reliance on imported protein sources. Governments can achieve this by creating incentives for producers to supply domestic markets, such as subsidies, tax breaks, or preferential market access for locally distributed products.

Aquaculture's integration into food strategies extends to rural development initiatives, as many small-scale farmers and fishers depend on it for their livelihoods. National food policies that support smallholder aquaculture through technical training, financial assistance, and infrastructure development contribute to food security while enhancing rural incomes. These efforts not only increase local production capacity but also empower communities to meet their own nutritional needs sustainably. Additionally, small-scale aquaculture can be integrated with other agricultural activities, such as rice-fish farming, to optimize resource use and diversify food production systems.

Another critical component of aligning aquaculture with food strategies is addressing resource efficiency and environmental sustainability. Aquaculture requires careful management of water, land, and feed resources to minimize environmental impacts and ensure long-term productivity. National food strategies should promote sustainable practices, such as RAS, IMTA, and the use of alternative feed sources. These practices reduce resource use, lower production costs, and enhance the sector's resilience to environmental changes, aligning with broader sustainability goals in food systems.

Collaboration across government ministries and agencies is essential for effective policy alignment. Aquaculture often intersects with multiple sectors, including agriculture, fisheries, water management, and public health. Coordinated planning and communication among these sectors ensure that aquaculture development aligns with national priorities and avoids conflicts over resource allocation. For instance, policies that integrate aquaculture with agricultural water use or irrigation systems can enhance efficiency and reduce competition for scarce resources.

Research and data collection are vital for aligning aquaculture with food strategies. Reliable data on production, consumption, and nutritional contributions of farmed aquatic products enable policymakers to make informed decisions and set realistic targets. National food strategies can support research on aquaculture's role in meeting dietary needs, its environmental impacts, and its socioeconomic benefits. By identifying gaps and opportunities, this research informs policies that maximize aquaculture's contributions to food security.

Education and public awareness campaigns also play a role in integrating aquaculture into food strategies. These initiatives help consumers understand the nutritional value and sustainability of farmed aquatic products, increasing demand and supporting local production. Public awareness efforts can also address misconceptions about aquaculture practices and build trust in the sector, fostering a positive perception of farmed seafood as a critical component of national food systems.

Addressing challenges such as market access, resource competition, and climate change is integral to successful alignment. National food strategies must incorporate adaptive measures to ensure that aquaculture remains resilient in the face of changing environmental and economic conditions. Policies that encourage innovation, such as investments in technology and capacity building, can help the sector adapt to challenges while maintaining its contributions to food security.

By aligning aquaculture with national food strategies, countries can create synergies between the sector's potential and broader food security objectives. This integration enhances nutrition, supports livelihoods, and contributes to sustainable development, positioning aquaculture as a cornerstone of resilient and inclusive food systems.

6.3.2. Cross-sectoral Collaboration for Resilience

Cross-sectoral collaboration is essential for building resilience in aquaculture, ensuring that the sector can adapt to environmental, social, and economic challenges while contributing effectively to food security. By fostering partnerships between governments, private industry, research institutions, and local communities, cross-sectoral collaboration enhances resource efficiency, innovation, and the sustainable development of aquaculture systems. This approach not only strengthens aquaculture's role in food security but also aligns it with broader goals in climate adaptation, rural development, and economic resilience.

One of the primary areas where cross-sectoral collaboration is critical is resource management. Aquaculture operations often depend on shared resources such as water, land, and feed, creating potential conflicts with other sectors, including agriculture, fisheries, and urban development. Collaborative planning ensures that resource use is optimized and equitably distributed. For example, partnerships between the aquaculture and agriculture sectors can promote integrated farming systems, such as aquaponics or rice-fish farming, which maximize the use of water and nutrients while diversifying food production. Joint resource management frameworks help balance competing demands and mitigate conflicts, particularly in regions where water scarcity or land-use pressures are significant.

Climate change adaptation is another area where cross-sectoral collaboration plays a pivotal role. Rising temperatures, changing precipitation patterns, and extreme weather events pose significant risks to aquaculture operations, particularly in coastal and low-lying areas. Collaboration between aquaculture stakeholders, climate scientists, and policymakers enables the development of strategies to mitigate these risks. For instance, coastal aquaculture operations can partner with environmental agencies to restore mangroves and wetlands, which act as natural buffers against storm surges and sea-level rise. Similarly, partnerships with renewable energy providers can support the adoption of solar- or wind-powered aquaculture systems, reducing carbon emissions and increasing resilience to energy price fluctuations.

Research and innovation are at the heart of cross-sectoral collaboration for building aquaculture resilience. Partnerships between academic institutions, industry stakeholders, and government agencies facilitate the development and dissemination of technologies that improve productivity and sustainability. For example, advancements in alternative feeds, such as insect- or algae-based formulations, address the sector's reliance on fishmeal and fish oil, reducing pressure on wild fish stocks. Collaborative research initiatives also drive the development of disease-resistant strains, precision farming technologies, and advanced water filtration systems, ensuring that aquaculture remains competitive and sustainable in the face of emerging challenges.

Economic resilience is enhanced through collaboration with financial institutions and development organizations. Access to affordable credit, insurance, and investment capital is essential for aquaculture producers to recover from disruptions and invest in sustainable practices. PPPs play a key role in providing financial support and reducing risk for small-scale farmers and entrepreneurs. For example, joint funding programs can support the establishment of cooperatives, allowing smallholders to pool resources, access markets, and adopt innovative technologies. These partnerships strengthen the economic foundation of the aquaculture sector, enabling it to withstand shocks and contribute to national food security goals.

Education and capacity building are also critical components of cross-sectoral collaboration. Training programs and knowledge-sharing platforms bring together stakeholders from different sectors to build skills and awareness of best practices. For instance, extension services that connect aquaculture producers with agricultural experts can enhance understanding of integrated farming systems and resource conservation. Collaborative training initiatives also help local communities and small-scale farmers adopt sustainable practices, improving their livelihoods and ensuring long-term resilience.

Policy alignment is another important dimension of cross-sectoral collaboration. Aquaculture intersects with numerous policy domains, including environmental management, public health, trade, and rural development. Coordinating policies across these areas ensures that aquaculture development aligns with national and international goals. For example, integrating aquaculture into national climate adaptation plans or rural development strategies ensures that the sector receives the necessary support to address emerging challenges while contributing to broader sustainability objectives.

Despite its benefits, fostering cross-sectoral collaboration can be challenging due to differing priorities, resource constraints, and institutional barriers. Effective communication and governance mechanisms are essential for overcoming these challenges. Multi-stakeholder platforms, such as regional aquaculture networks or advisory councils, provide forums for dialogue and decision-making, ensuring that all voices are heard and that collaboration efforts are inclusive and transparent.

Cross-sectoral collaboration is indispensable for building resilience in aquaculture, enabling the sector to adapt to dynamic conditions and enhance its contributions to food security. By bringing together diverse stakeholders, leveraging collective expertise, and fostering innovation, collaboration ensures that aquaculture systems are equipped to navigate complex challenges while supporting sustainable and equitable development.

Chapter 7: Economic Potential of Aquaculture

Aquaculture has become a cornerstone of global food systems, offering significant economic opportunities for nations and communities alike. This chapter examines the economic potential of aquaculture, focusing on its contributions to global trade, employment, and rural development. By exploring financial mechanisms, market trends, and economic strategies, this chapter highlights how aquaculture can be harnessed to foster sustainable growth, improve livelihoods, and strengthen economies around the world.

7.1. Global Trade and Economic Impact

Global trade in aquaculture products plays a vital role in the industry's economic impact, driving growth, creating jobs, and contributing significantly to the economies of both producing and importing countries.

7.1.1. Contributions of Aquaculture to GDP in Key Producing Nations

Aquaculture has become a significant contributor to the gross domestic product (GDP) of many nations, particularly those with large, developed aquaculture sectors. As the global demand for seafood continues to rise, aquaculture has emerged as a key economic engine, not only providing a sustainable source of food but also generating income, employment, and export revenue. In countries with well-established aquaculture industries, such as China, Norway, and Vietnam, aquaculture's contribution to GDP is substantial and continues to grow as the sector expands to meet global needs.

China: The Global Leader in Aquaculture Production

China is by far the largest producer of aquaculture products in the world, accounting for more than 60% of global production. The country's aquaculture sector plays a crucial role in its economy, contributing significantly to both rural development and national GDP. As of recent estimates, aquaculture accounts for around 1.5% of China's total GDP, a figure that is even higher in rural areas where aquaculture is a major source of income. The sector generates millions of jobs, from small-scale pond farming to large-scale commercial operations, and serves as a vital food source for China's vast population.

The Chinese government has played a key role in supporting aquaculture's growth, investing in research, infrastructure, and market development. The country's robust aquaculture industry not only feeds domestic markets but also provides a substantial portion of global seafood exports. In recent years, China has increasingly focused on improving the sustainability of its aquaculture practices through technological innovation and environmental management, further solidifying its role in the global market.

Norway: A Leader in Sustainable Seafood Exports

Norway, with its cold-water coastal regions and highly developed infrastructure, has become one of the world's largest exporters of farmed salmon. Aquaculture accounts for a significant portion of Norway's GDP, particularly within the seafood industry. In fact, seafood, including farmed fish, is one of the country's largest export sectors, contributing billions of dollars to the national economy each year. The total value of aquaculture's contribution to GDP in Norway is estimated to be around 2-3%, with the salmon farming sector alone accounting for over 10% of total exports.

Norway's success in aquaculture is attributed to a combination of factors, including access to clean water, a strong regulatory framework for sustainability, and technological advancements in fish farming systems. The country is a global leader in producing high-quality farmed salmon, with the majority of its production destined for international markets. As global demand for seafood continues to rise, Norway's aquaculture sector is positioned for continued growth, further contributing to its national GDP and supporting thousands of jobs in rural coastal communities.

Vietnam: Aquaculture as a Key Economic Driver

Vietnam, one of the largest exporters of farmed shrimp and pangasius, also benefits significantly from its aquaculture sector. Aquaculture contributes around 3-4% of Vietnam's total GDP and is a critical component of the country's agricultural sector. The aquaculture industry provides livelihoods for millions of people, particularly in rural and coastal areas, where fish and shrimp farming are among the most important economic activities.

Vietnam's success in aquaculture is largely driven by its competitive advantage in producing farmed shrimp and catfish, which are in high demand in international markets. The sector's rapid growth has been supported by favorable government policies, international trade agreements, and investments in infrastructure, such as improved farming techniques and processing plants. With a strong focus on exports, particularly to markets in the United States, Europe, and Asia, Vietnam's aquaculture industry continues to contribute significantly to both the country's GDP and its trade balance.

India: Growing Potential in Aquaculture

India, with its vast coastline and access to freshwater resources, has considerable potential for aquaculture development. Aquaculture currently accounts for about 1.5% of India's GDP, with a significant portion of production coming from freshwater species like carp. India is also one of the largest producers of farmed shrimp, particularly in coastal regions such as Andhra Pradesh, which has led to significant growth in the shrimp export market.

The Indian government has made aquaculture a priority under its national agricultural policies, recognizing its potential to generate employment and boost rural incomes. With continued investment in infrastructure, technology, and market access, India's aquaculture sector is expected to see continued growth, further enhancing its contribution to the national GDP. As global demand for seafood continues to increase, India is well-positioned to expand its aquaculture production and strengthen its economic standing in the global seafood market.

Other Key Producers

Several other countries also derive significant economic benefits from aquaculture, including Thailand, Chile, and Indonesia. Thailand, with its shrimp farming sector, is a major player in the global seafood market, and aquaculture contributes substantially to the country's agricultural GDP. Chile, known for its salmon farming industry, is one of the largest exporters of farmed fish in Latin America, and aquaculture remains a critical part of its economic strategy. In Indonesia, aquaculture is growing rapidly, contributing to job creation, rural development, and food security, particularly in the form of freshwater fish farming.

In all of these countries, the economic contributions of aquaculture are increasingly recognized as vital to national development, rural livelihoods, and food security. As global seafood demand continues to rise and sustainable practices are adopted, the economic impact of aquaculture will likely expand, further integrating the sector into national economies and global trade networks.

7.1.2. Export Trends and Trade Dynamics in the Aquaculture Sector

The aquaculture sector has become an essential component of global trade, with exports of farmed seafood contributing significantly to the economies of producing countries and satisfying the rising global demand for protein-rich food sources. The dynamics of aquaculture exports are shaped by various factors, including consumer preferences, technological advancements, regulatory standards, and shifts in global supply chains. This section explores key trends and trade dynamics in the global aquaculture market, focusing on export volumes, emerging markets, and the evolving role of aquaculture in international trade.

Increasing Global Demand for Aquaculture Products

The global demand for seafood has been steadily increasing, driven by population growth, rising incomes, and shifting dietary patterns. Aquaculture has been essential in meeting this demand, accounting for over 50% of the world's seafood production. With fish and shellfish being important sources of protein, particularly in developing countries, aquaculture is seen as a sustainable solution to address food security challenges while reducing pressure on wild fisheries.

As consumer preferences shift toward more sustainable and traceable food sources, demand for responsibly farmed aquaculture products is also increasing. This has led to a surge in the adoption of certification programs, such as the ASC and Global GAP, which ensure that farmed seafood is produced with minimal environmental impact. These certifications have helped aquaculture products command higher prices in key export markets, such as the EU, North America, and Japan.

Major Exporting Countries

Countries with well-established aquaculture industries, such as China, Norway, Vietnam, Chile, and Thailand, dominate global exports of farmed seafood. China remains the world's largest producer and exporter of aquaculture products, accounting for more than 60% of global production. The country's export volumes are primarily driven by its production of farmed fish, shellfish, and processed seafood products. Although China also imports significant quantities of seafood for processing and re-export, its export sector remains a critical player in the global seafood trade.

Norway is another leading exporter, particularly of farmed salmon. Salmon farming is a cornerstone of Norway's aquaculture industry, and the country accounts for more than 50% of global salmon exports. In recent years, Norway has maintained a strong competitive position in the international market due to its focus on sustainable farming practices, advanced technology, and access to clean, cold waters. Norwegian salmon is highly valued for its high quality, and the country has expanded its reach to new markets in Asia, the Middle East, and Latin America.

Vietnam, as one of the largest producers of farmed shrimp and pangasius, has also seen significant growth in its aquaculture export sector. The country's shrimp and catfish farms benefit from its extensive coastline, low labor costs, and relatively simple production systems, making it highly competitive in the global market. The EU, the United States, and Japan are key destinations for Vietnamese aquaculture products, and the country continues to diversify its offerings by incorporating value-added products such as processed shrimp and frozen fish.

Chile is a leading exporter of farmed salmon in Latin America, benefiting from its favorable coastal conditions and regulatory framework that supports sustainable farming practices. As the global appetite for salmon continues to grow, Chile's export volumes have risen, with major markets including the EU, North America, and emerging markets in Asia. Similarly, Thailand's shrimp farming sector remains a major contributor to the country's export revenue, with shrimp being one of the top aquaculture exports, particularly to the United States, Japan, and the EU.

Emerging Markets and Shifting Trade Dynamics

The dynamics of aquaculture exports are shifting as new markets emerge, and traditional trade relationships evolve. Countries in Asia,

Africa, and the Middle East are increasing their consumption of farmed seafood due to rising incomes and changing dietary preferences. These emerging markets represent an important growth opportunity for exporters, particularly for countries with established aquaculture sectors like China, Vietnam, and Thailand.

India, for example, is gradually expanding its aquaculture exports, particularly in the form of shrimp and freshwater species. The government has made efforts to boost the country's competitiveness in the global market through initiatives like improving production systems, enhancing infrastructure, and securing market access for Indian seafood products. India's growing shrimp export sector, in particular, has made significant inroads in the United States and Europe, competing with established suppliers like Ecuador and Vietnam.

Meanwhile, the European Union and the United States remain key markets for aquaculture exports, but trade dynamics are changing due to new consumer preferences for sustainably sourced seafood. As a result, the importance of certifications and traceability in aquaculture exports has risen, driving both producers and exporters to adopt more sustainable practices to meet the growing demand for eco-friendly products. Countries that are able to meet stringent environmental and social criteria are likely to gain a competitive advantage in these high-value markets.

Furthermore, there has been an increase in intra-regional trade within Asia and Africa. Countries such as Indonesia, the Philippines, and Malaysia are strengthening their intra-Asian trade in farmed fish, shrimp, and mollusks, taking advantage of proximity, lower transportation costs, and growing regional demand for seafood. This shift is expected to continue, particularly as regional free trade agreements and the growing middle class in emerging markets further stimulate demand for farmed seafood.

Challenges and Opportunities

While the global aquaculture export market presents significant opportunities, it also faces challenges such as trade barriers, environmental concerns, and competition from wild-caught seafood. Tariffs, trade restrictions, and the use of antidumping measures can disrupt market access and affect the profitability of exporting nations. Moreover, the sustainability of aquaculture practices remains a key issue, with increasing pressure on producers to minimize environmental impacts such as water pollution and disease outbreaks.

Nonetheless, the growing demand for sustainable and responsibly sourced seafood offers significant opportunities for aquaculture exporters who can meet these consumer preferences. Investments in sustainable farming practices, technological innovation, and value-added products, such as fillets and processed seafood, can provide exporters with a competitive edge in both traditional and emerging markets.

In conclusion, export trends and trade dynamics in the aquaculture sector are shaped by evolving consumer preferences, market competition, and the demand for sustainable seafood. As global trade in aquaculture products continues to grow, key exporting nations will need to adapt to shifting market conditions and prioritize sustainability to maintain their competitive positions.

7.2. Financial Mechanisms for Aquaculture Growth

Financial mechanisms play a crucial role in supporting the growth and sustainability of the aquaculture sector by providing the necessary capital, risk management tools, and investment incentives to foster innovation, expansion, and environmental responsibility.

7.2.1. Public and Private Investments in Aquaculture

Public and private investments are critical drivers of growth and innovation in the aquaculture sector. The industry requires significant capital to address challenges such as resource efficiency, environmental sustainability, and market access, while also expanding to meet the rising global demand for seafood. Investments from both the public and private sectors contribute to technological advancements, infrastructure development, and capacity building, helping to ensure that aquaculture remains a viable and sustainable solution for food security. This section explores the role of both public and private investments in shaping the future of aquaculture.

Public Investments in Aquaculture

Public investment plays a central role in supporting the aquaculture industry, particularly in developing countries where access to capital may be limited. Governments provide funding for aquaculture research, infrastructure, training, and policy development to help boost production capacity, enhance food security, and address environmental challenges. In many cases, public funding is directed toward sectors that are crucial for the broader national economy, such as rural development and employment generation.

One of the main areas where public investments have a significant impact is in research and development (R&D). Public sector funding enables research institutions and universities to develop innovative solutions that improve aquaculture practices, such as disease prevention, feed efficiency, and environmental management. Governments often collaborate with research organizations and the private sector to tackle industry-wide challenges, ensuring that new technologies and practices can be scaled and adopted across the sector. For instance, many governments fund aquaculture R&D programs aimed at improving the sustainability of feed production, reducing reliance on wild fish stocks, and minimizing the environmental footprint of aquaculture operations.

Infrastructure development is another key area where public investments contribute to aquaculture growth. Governments invest in infrastructure such as hatcheries, processing facilities, and transportation networks to improve the efficiency and competitiveness of the aquaculture industry. These investments are essential for creating the necessary infrastructure to support both large-scale commercial operations and smallholder farmers. For example, the construction of cold storage facilities and efficient transport systems helps reduce post-harvest losses and ensures that aquaculture products reach consumers in optimal condition.

Additionally, public investments are often directed toward improving the regulatory and policy framework surrounding aquaculture. By providing subsidies, grants, and low-interest loans, governments incentivize sustainable practices in the sector and encourage investment in environmentally friendly technologies. For example, public funding may support the development of eco-friendly RAS or integrated multi-trophic aquaculture systems that reduce waste and improve resource efficiency. By creating favorable policy environments, governments can encourage both domestic and foreign investment in aquaculture while also addressing environmental and social concerns.

Private Investments in Aquaculture

Private sector investments in aquaculture have been increasingly important, especially as the industry has become more commercialized and globalized. Private investors, ranging from individual entrepreneurs to multinational corporations, provide capital for aquaculture businesses, helping them scale operations, adopt new technologies, and expand into new markets. The private sector is particularly adept at bringing innovation to the industry, driving advancements in technology, feed production, and sustainable farming practices.

One of the most significant areas of private investment in aquaculture is in the development of new aquaculture technologies. Private companies invest in innovations that improve productivity, reduce costs, and enhance sustainability. For example, investment in automated feeding systems, which are integrated with sensors and AI, helps aquaculture farms optimize feed use, improve growth rates, and reduce waste. Such innovations not only benefit aquaculture businesses by lowering operational costs but also contribute to broader environmental goals by reducing the environmental impact of farming practices.

Another area of private investment is in the development of alternative protein sources for aquaculture feed. The global aquaculture industry has faced challenges in sourcing sustainable feed ingredients, particularly as demand for fishmeal and fish oil continues to outpace supply. Private companies are investing in the development of plant-based and insect-based feed ingredients, which offer more sustainable and cost-effective alternatives to traditional feed sources. These innovations are key to ensuring the long-term sustainability of the sector and addressing concerns about overfishing and pressure on wild fish stocks.

Private investments also play a critical role in the expansion of aquaculture farms and processing facilities. Investors in large-scale aquaculture operations can provide the necessary capital to build the infrastructure needed to increase production capacity, create jobs, and improve the efficiency of the sector. As the demand for seafood continues to rise, private investors are supporting the construction of state-of-the-art fish farming facilities, such as offshore aquaculture systems and land-based recirculating systems, that can produce large quantities of high-quality seafood in an environmentally sustainable manner.

Furthermore, private investors are crucial in expanding the global aquaculture market. By investing in international expansion, private companies can tap into growing markets for farmed seafood in regions such as Asia, the Middle East, and Latin America. As the global demand for seafood continues to rise, private sector investments in market development and distribution networks enable aquaculture producers to meet consumer demand across the world.

Public-Private Partnerships

In many cases, the public and private sectors work together to advance the aquaculture industry through PPPs. These partnerships combine the strengths of both sectors, with governments providing policy support, infrastructure, and funding, while the private sector brings innovation, efficiency, and capital. PPPs are particularly effective in developing countries, where public funding may be insufficient to support the entire aquaculture value chain. By leveraging both public and private resources, PPPs can address challenges such as access to markets, infrastructure development, and environmental sustainability.

For example, in some regions, PPPs have been instrumental in developing eco-friendly aquaculture systems that reduce the environmental impact of farming practices while improving productivity. Such partnerships often involve government agencies, NGOs, and private companies collaborating to design and implement projects that balance economic, social, and environmental objectives.

Public and private investments are vital to the growth and sustainability of the aquaculture industry. Public sector investments provide essential infrastructure, research, and regulatory support, while private sector investments bring innovation, technological advancements, and capital to the industry. Through strategic collaboration, both sectors can create a resilient and sustainable aquaculture sector capable of meeting the growing global demand for seafood.

7.2.2. Role of Microfinance and Cooperatives in Small-Scale Aquaculture

Microfinance and cooperatives play a vital role in the development and sustainability of small-scale aquaculture operations, particularly in developing countries where access to capital and resources can be limited. These financial tools help empower smallholder farmers, improve their productivity, and enable them to participate in the growing global aquaculture market. By providing affordable financial services and creating opportunities for collective action, microfinance institutions and cooperatives are critical in fostering economic growth, food security, and environmental sustainability at the grassroots level.

Microfinance and its Impact on Small-Scale Aquaculture

Microfinance refers to the provision of small loans and financial services to individuals or small enterprises that do not have access to traditional banking services. For small-scale aquaculture farmers, microfinance offers a way to obtain the capital needed to invest in aquaculture infrastructure, improve production practices, and overcome financial barriers. These loans can be used for a variety of purposes, including purchasing equipment, stocking ponds, improving water quality management systems, or investing in feed and other inputs. Microfinance institutions (MFIs) typically offer small loans with lower interest rates, flexible repayment schedules, and minimal collateral requirements, making it easier for smallholders to access the necessary funds for their operations.

In many developing countries, small-scale aquaculture plays a significant role in rural economies, providing livelihoods for millions of people. However, small-scale farmers often face challenges such as limited access to capital, which hinders their ability to scale operations, adopt new technologies, or improve the sustainability of their farms. Microfinance fills this gap by offering tailored financial products that cater to the specific needs of aquaculture farmers. For example, loans can help farmers improve their aquaculture systems through the purchase of modern equipment, such as aerators or filtration systems, which can enhance productivity and reduce costs in the long term.

In addition to loans, many microfinance institutions provide training and capacity-building programs to ensure that borrowers are equipped with the necessary skills to effectively manage their aquaculture operations. These programs often cover essential topics such as financial literacy, business management, sustainable farming practices, and environmental stewardship. By improving the financial and technical capacity of farmers, microfinance institutions help ensure that small-scale aquaculture operations are more resilient and productive, ultimately contributing to greater food security and economic stability for rural communities.

Cooperatives and Collective Action in Small-Scale Aquaculture

Cooperatives are another important mechanism for supporting small-scale aquaculture. A cooperative is an organization owned and operated by its members, who share in the profits and responsibilities of the business. In the context of aquaculture, cooperatives provide a platform for smallholder farmers to pool resources, access better market opportunities, and achieve economies of scale. By working together, farmers can reduce costs, increase bargaining power, and share knowledge and best practices, which can lead to improved productivity and sustainability.

One of the main benefits of cooperatives in small-scale aquaculture is the ability to collectively purchase inputs, such as feed, equipment, and fingerlings, at lower prices. By aggregating demand, cooperatives can negotiate bulk discounts, reducing the cost of production for individual farmers. Additionally, cooperatives often provide shared access to equipment, such as hatcheries or processing facilities, which might otherwise be too expensive for individual farmers to invest in. This collective approach enables small-scale farmers to overcome financial barriers, increase production capacity, and improve the quality of their products.

Cooperatives also play a crucial role in improving market access for smallholder aquaculture farmers. In many cases, small-scale farmers face challenges in accessing markets for their products due to limited transportation, lack of market information, and the inability to meet market standards. By pooling resources and organizing collective marketing efforts, cooperatives can help farmers reach larger and more lucrative markets. Cooperatives can also assist with product certification, such as organic or fair-trade certification, which can increase the market value of farmed seafood and provide access to premium markets.

In addition to improving market access, cooperatives also provide a platform for farmers to share knowledge and best practices. Through training programs, workshops, and peer-to-peer learning, cooperative members can exchange information on sustainable farming techniques, pest and disease management, and water quality control. This collaborative approach helps farmers adopt more efficient and environmentally friendly practices, improving the sustainability of small-scale aquaculture operations.

Moreover, cooperatives are often involved in advocacy and policy engagement, helping smallholder farmers voice their concerns and secure support from governments and international organizations. By representing the collective interests of their members, cooperatives can influence policies related to aquaculture development, such as access to credit, subsidies, and regulations. This advocacy helps create a more favorable policy environment for small-scale aquaculture and ensures that the needs of smallholder farmers are considered in national and regional development strategies.

The Synergy Between Microfinance and Cooperatives

The combination of microfinance and cooperatives creates a powerful support system for small-scale aquaculture. Microfinance institutions provide the financial capital needed to start or expand aquaculture operations, while cooperatives offer a platform for collective action, resource pooling, and market access. Together, they enable smallholder farmers to overcome financial and operational challenges, increase their production capacity, and improve the sustainability of their operations.

In many cases, microfinance institutions and cooperatives work together to support small-scale aquaculture development. For example, microfinance institutions may partner with cooperatives to provide loans and financial services to cooperative members. This collaboration ensures that smallholders have access to both capital and the collective resources offered by cooperatives, increasing the likelihood of success for individual farmers and the cooperative as a whole.

Overall, microfinance and cooperatives are essential tools for empowering small-scale aquaculture farmers, improving their access to capital, resources, and markets, and promoting sustainable practices. By providing financial support, technical assistance, and a platform for collective action, these mechanisms help smallholder farmers thrive in a competitive and evolving aquaculture industry, ultimately contributing to food security and rural development.

Chapter 8. The Future of Aquaculture in Food Security

As the global population continues to grow and the demand for sustainable food sources intensifies, aquaculture is poised to play an increasingly vital role in ensuring food security worldwide. This chapter explores the future of aquaculture, examining emerging trends, technological innovations, and policy developments that will shape its capacity to address the challenges of food production, environmental sustainability, and economic resilience. By focusing on the evolving landscape of the aquaculture industry, we highlight how it can contribute to a more secure, sustainable, and equitable global food system in the coming decades.

8.1. Challenges Ahead for Aquaculture

As aquaculture continues to expand to meet global food demands, it faces a range of challenges that must be addressed to ensure its sustainability, including environmental impacts, resource limitations, and changing market dynamics.

8.1.1. Climate Change Impacts on Aquaculture Systems

Climate change poses significant risks to aquaculture systems, affecting both freshwater and marine environments where aquaculture operations are based. As global temperatures rise, weather patterns become more erratic, and ocean conditions change, aquaculture systems are increasingly vulnerable to disruptions that could affect the productivity, sustainability, and economic viability of the sector.

One of the primary concerns for aquaculture due to climate change is the warming of water temperatures. Most aquaculture species have specific temperature ranges in which they thrive. As water temperatures increase, many species may experience heat stress, which can reduce growth rates, reproductive success, and overall health. For instance, farmed salmon, which are sensitive to changes in water temperature, can suffer from higher mortality rates and reduced growth performance as ocean temperatures rise. In areas where water temperature increases beyond the optimal range, aquaculture operations may be forced to either adapt by switching to different species or face reduced yields and economic losses.

In addition to warming water temperatures, climate change is contributing to ocean acidification, which occurs as excess carbon dioxide (CO_2) is absorbed by seawater, lowering its pH. This shift in ocean chemistry can negatively affect the growth and development of marine species such as shellfish and coral, which rely on calcium carbonate to form their shells and structures. For aquaculture systems, this means that shellfish farms may see slower growth rates and weakened shells, making them more vulnerable to disease and predation. In the long term, ocean acidification could impact the viability of shellfish farming, particularly in areas where the pH levels of seawater have dropped significantly.

Changes in precipitation patterns and the increased frequency of extreme weather events are also problematic for aquaculture systems. Droughts, floods, and storms can disrupt the availability and quality of water, especially in land-based or freshwater aquaculture systems. For example, heavy rainfall can lead to runoff from agricultural areas, carrying pollutants and sediment into aquaculture ponds, which can degrade water quality and increase the risk of disease. On the other hand, drought conditions can reduce the availability of water for aquaculture operations, particularly in regions where freshwater resources are already stressed.

Moreover, the rise in sea levels due to climate change poses a threat to coastal aquaculture operations, such as those found in shrimp farming and shellfish production. Coastal flooding and increased salinity can damage infrastructure, contaminate water sources, and reduce the amount of suitable land for farming. In areas vulnerable to sea level rise, aquaculture farms may need to invest in costly infrastructure upgrades or relocate to higher ground, increasing operational costs and reducing profitability.

Overall, climate change impacts on aquaculture systems are complex and multifaceted, affecting everything from species health to infrastructure stability. As the industry adapts to these challenges, it will require innovation in farming practices, breeding techniques, and environmental management to ensure that aquaculture continues to play a role in global food security.

8.1.2. Balancing Growth with Sustainability

As global demand for seafood continues to rise, aquaculture faces the critical challenge of balancing growth with sustainability. The need for increased production must be reconciled with the imperative to reduce the environmental footprint of aquaculture operations and ensure the long-term viability of ecosystems. Achieving this balance requires adopting innovative farming practices, improving resource efficiency, and addressing the sector's environmental impacts without compromising productivity.

One of the central sustainability concerns in aquaculture is the efficient use of resources, particularly water, feed, and energy. Traditional aquaculture systems, especially those relying on open-net cages, can contribute to significant environmental degradation, including water pollution, habitat destruction, and the depletion of wild fish stocks used in feed production. To meet the growing demand for seafood, the industry must shift towards more sustainable systems. Technologies like RAS and IMTA hold promise in reducing the environmental impact of aquaculture. RAS systems, for instance, recycle water within a closed system, reducing water usage and minimizing effluent discharge into the environment. This approach also allows for better control of water quality, reducing the need for chemicals and antibiotics. Similarly, IMTA integrates multiple species in the same system, with different species feeding off one another's by-products, improving resource utilization and reducing waste.

The development of alternative feed ingredients is another crucial area for balancing growth with sustainability. Fishmeal and fish oil, traditionally sourced from wild fish stocks, are in limited supply and their overuse contributes to the depletion of marine ecosystems. Sustainable aquaculture practices are increasingly relying on plant-based or insect-based protein sources for fish feed. Innovations in feed production, including the use of algae, soy, and micro-organisms, offer the potential to reduce dependence on wild-caught fish and lower the ecological footprint of the industry. However, the challenge remains to develop cost-effective and nutritionally balanced feeds that can sustain the health and growth of farmed species.

The efficient use of energy is also a key consideration in sustainable aquaculture. As the industry grows, energy consumption for operations, particularly in intensive systems, will increase. Moving towards renewable energy sources, such as solar and wind, can help reduce the carbon footprint of aquaculture operations. By utilizing clean energy technologies, aquaculture can lower its greenhouse gas emissions, contributing to broader climate change mitigation efforts.

Ultimately, balancing growth with sustainability in aquaculture is about fostering practices that allow the industry to expand while minimizing its environmental impact. This balance requires investment in technology, innovation in feed and farming practices, and collaboration between the private sector, governments, and environmental organizations to ensure that aquaculture can meet global seafood demands without compromising future generations' ability to produce food sustainably.

8.2. Opportunities for Transformative Growth

The aquaculture industry faces significant opportunities for transformative growth, driven by technological innovations, sustainable practices, and evolving market demands that can shape its future as a key solution to global food security challenges.

8.2.1. Innovation in Sustainable Practices

117

Innovation in sustainable practices is central to the future growth of aquaculture, enabling the industry to meet increasing demand for seafood while minimizing its environmental impact. As the global population grows and pressures on natural resources intensify, there is a critical need for aquaculture to evolve in ways that balance productivity with ecological stewardship. Technological advancements, improved farming techniques, and sustainable feed solutions are transforming aquaculture, making it more environmentally responsible and resilient in the face of climate change and resource constraints.

One of the most significant innovations in sustainable aquaculture is the development of RAS. RAS allows for water to be continuously filtered and reused within a closed-loop system, significantly reducing water consumption and preventing effluent discharge into the environment. This system is particularly beneficial in areas where water is scarce or where open-net farming may lead to pollution of natural water bodies. By creating a controlled environment, RAS can also improve fish health by maintaining optimal water conditions, reducing the need for antibiotics and chemicals. The ability to recycle water and manage waste effectively makes RAS one of the most environmentally sustainable technologies in modern aquaculture.

Another key innovation is IMTA, which mimics natural ecosystems by cultivating multiple species from different trophic levels within the same system. For example, fish, shellfish, and seaweed are farmed together, where the waste produced by one species becomes a resource for another. Fish waste can provide nutrients for algae and shellfish, which, in turn, can improve water quality and help filter excess nutrients. This symbiotic approach not only maximizes resource efficiency but also reduces the environmental burden typically associated with monoculture farming. IMTA has the potential to increase the sustainability of coastal aquaculture operations by reducing the need for artificial fertilizers, improving water quality, and mitigating the impact of nutrient pollution.

In addition to innovative farming systems, alternative feed ingredients are a critical area of innovation. Traditional fish feed relies heavily on wild-caught fishmeal and fish oil, leading to concerns about the sustainability of marine ecosystems. Innovations in feed ingredients, such as plant-based proteins, insect meal, and algae, offer sustainable alternatives that reduce the pressure on wild fish stocks. For instance, microalgae can be used to produce high-quality, omega-3-rich feed that is nutritionally equivalent to traditional fish oil, offering a more sustainable option. Insects, such as black soldier fly larvae, are also being explored as a high-protein, low-cost feed source that can be produced with minimal environmental impact. These alternative feed solutions not only support sustainable aquaculture practices but also help reduce the industry's carbon footprint.

Furthermore, the use of smart technologies in aquaculture farming is transforming how operations are managed, improving efficiency, and reducing waste. The integration of sensors, AI, and IoT technologies allows farmers to monitor water quality, fish health, and feed consumption in real-time, enabling more precise control over farming operations. Automated feeding systems, for example, help reduce feed waste by ensuring that fish receive the right amount of food at the right time, while smart sensors can detect changes in water quality, allowing for early intervention to prevent disease outbreaks.

These innovations in sustainable practices offer a glimpse into the future of aquaculture, where efficiency, productivity, and environmental stewardship are inextricably linked. By adopting and scaling these technologies, the aquaculture industry can continue to grow while minimizing its environmental impact and contributing to global food security. As the demand for sustainable seafood increases, innovation will be the key to transforming aquaculture into a truly sustainable industry that can meet the needs of both consumers and the planet.

8.2.2. Collaboration Across Sectors

Collaboration across sectors is essential for the future growth and sustainability of the aquaculture industry. As the demand for seafood increases, the aquaculture sector must adapt to meet this demand while minimizing its environmental footprint and ensuring social and economic benefits. No single entity or sector can solve the complex challenges facing aquaculture alone. Instead, a collaborative approach involving government agencies, private companies, research institutions, and local communities is necessary to promote sustainable growth, innovation, and resilience.

One of the most significant areas for collaboration is in R&D. Governments, private enterprises, and academic institutions are increasingly working together to fund and conduct R&D projects aimed at improving aquaculture practices. PPPs have become a key model for driving innovation in sustainable aquaculture. For example, companies in the feed industry, working with universities and government bodies, are developing alternative, plant-based proteins for aquaculture feed that reduce reliance on wild-caught fish. These collaborations allow for the pooling of resources, expertise, and data, accelerating the development of new technologies and practices that improve efficiency and sustainability.

Similarly, environmental organizations and aquaculture producers are working together to create sustainable production methods that minimize negative ecological impacts. For instance, non-governmental organizations (NGOs) and environmental advocacy groups collaborate with aquaculture farms to implement best practices that reduce pollution, such as integrated pest management or waste treatment systems. These collaborations not only help improve the environmental performance of aquaculture but also foster a positive image for the industry, building consumer confidence and driving demand for sustainably farmed seafood.

Another critical area for cross-sectoral collaboration is policy development and regulation. Governments, private industry, and advocacy groups must work together to create policies that support sustainable aquaculture growth while addressing issues like water use, environmental protection, and labor rights. Policymakers must collaborate with industry experts to ensure that regulations are effective and feasible while promoting innovation and growth. For example, policies that incentivize the adoption of sustainable technologies, such as tax breaks for farms that install RAS, can help accelerate the transition to more environmentally friendly farming practices. Likewise, international cooperation is needed to align regulations across borders to ensure sustainable and efficient global aquaculture trade.

The collaboration between local communities and aquaculture enterprises is also essential for ensuring that aquaculture contributes to rural development and food security. Community engagement helps aquaculture farms understand local needs and concerns, allowing for more socially responsible practices. It also provides local communities with opportunities to benefit from the industry, whether through direct employment or the development of related businesses, such as processing or distribution networks.

Finally, collaborative partnerships between aquaculture and other agricultural sectors can create synergies that optimize the use of resources and improve productivity. Integrated farming systems, such as rice-fish or agro-aquaculture systems, combine aquaculture with crop farming, benefiting both sectors. By using water from fish ponds to irrigate crops, for example, farmers can reduce water usage while increasing productivity in both aquaculture and agriculture. These cross-sectoral collaborations help build more resilient, diversified food production systems that contribute to food security.

In conclusion, collaboration across sectors is vital for the future of aquaculture. By leveraging the expertise, resources, and perspectives of various stakeholders, aquaculture can overcome challenges and capitalize on opportunities for sustainable growth. A collaborative approach ensures that aquaculture develops in a way that benefits the economy, society, and the environment, helping to meet the global demand for seafood while contributing to broader sustainability goals.

8.3. A Vision for Sustainable Aquaculture in Food Security

A vision for sustainable aquaculture in food security involves creating an industry that not only meets the growing global demand for seafood but also prioritizes environmental stewardship, social equity, and long-term resilience.

8.3.1. Long-Term Strategies for Scaling Aquaculture

Scaling aquaculture sustainably to meet the growing global demand for seafood requires a long-term, strategic approach that integrates environmental, economic, and social considerations. As the industry faces increasing pressure from population growth, climate change, and resource limitations, effective strategies must focus on increasing production efficiency, reducing environmental impacts, and enhancing the resilience of aquaculture systems. Several long-term strategies are essential for scaling aquaculture in a way that contributes to global food security while preserving natural resources.

One of the primary strategies for scaling aquaculture is the development and adoption of sustainable farming systems. Technologies such as RAS and IMTA are pivotal in reducing the environmental footprint of aquaculture operations. RAS, for instance, recycles water within a closed system, significantly reducing water usage and minimizing pollution. IMTA systems, which combine various species from different trophic levels in a single system, can improve resource efficiency by allowing one species' waste to become another's nutrient source. By scaling these technologies and improving their efficiency, aquaculture can significantly increase production while reducing its impact on natural ecosystems.

Alternative feed sources represent another critical long-term strategy for scaling aquaculture sustainably. Traditional aquaculture feeds rely heavily on fishmeal and fish oil derived from wild-caught fish, which places strain on marine resources. Innovations in plant-based and insect-based feeds offer a more sustainable alternative, reducing pressure on wild fish populations and improving feed efficiency. The development of high-quality, sustainable feeds that support the growth and health of farmed species will be essential for scaling aquaculture without exacerbating environmental degradation.

Another strategy involves enhancing aquaculture's resilience to climate change. As water temperatures rise, aquaculture species may experience stress, reducing growth and increasing susceptibility to disease. To mitigate these effects, long-term strategies must include breeding programs focused on developing species with better climate resilience, such as heat-resistant fish or disease-resistant strains. Additionally, farm management practices that reduce the reliance on external inputs, such as synthetic chemicals or antibiotics, will be essential for ensuring the industry can adapt to changing environmental conditions.

Finally, policy frameworks and international collaboration will be fundamental for scaling aquaculture sustainably. Governments, international organizations, and industry stakeholders must work together to create policies that incentivize sustainable practices, improve market access, and ensure fair resource distribution. By fostering global cooperation and investing in research and development, the aquaculture sector can scale responsibly, contributing to food security while minimizing environmental and social risks.

In conclusion, scaling aquaculture sustainably requires a multifaceted, long-term approach that prioritizes innovation, environmental stewardship, and resilience. By adopting sustainable farming systems, investing in alternative feeds, and developing climate-resilient species, the industry can meet future food security needs without compromising ecological balance.

8.3.2. Pathways to Global Food Security

Aquaculture has the potential to play a critical role in achieving global food security, particularly as the world faces rising population growth, changing dietary preferences, and the pressures of climate change. To fulfill this potential, aquaculture must evolve along pathways that focus on sustainable practices, equitable access to resources, and the efficient production of nutritious, affordable seafood. By addressing the challenges of the industry and embracing innovative approaches, aquaculture can become a central part of the global solution to hunger and malnutrition.

One essential pathway to global food security is increasing the production capacity of aquaculture systems while ensuring that growth is sustainable. This can be achieved by adopting advanced farming technologies, such as RAS and IMTA, which optimize resource use and minimize environmental impacts. RAS allows for water reuse and filtration, which drastically reduces the need for water and prevents effluent discharge into natural ecosystems, making it particularly useful in areas with limited freshwater resources. IMTA, which incorporates multiple species from different trophic levels, provides a more balanced ecosystem that reduces waste and improves overall resource efficiency. By scaling these technologies, aquaculture can increase its contribution to global seafood production without expanding the environmental footprint.

Sustainable feed innovations are also a key pathway to global food security. Traditional fish feed, which relies heavily on fishmeal and fish oil, is increasingly unsustainable due to the pressure it places on wild fish stocks. To ensure that aquaculture can continue to meet global seafood demand, there must be a shift towards alternative, sustainable feed ingredients. Plant-based proteins, insect meals, and microalgae are promising alternatives that can reduce dependency on marine resources. By investing in the research and development of these feed sources, the aquaculture industry can lower its environmental impact and enhance the sustainability of seafood production.

Furthermore, integrating aquaculture with other sectors, such as agriculture and nutrition, is vital for improving food security.

Integrated systems like rice-fish farming and agro-aquaculture offer benefits to both sectors, creating more diversified, resilient, and efficient food production systems. These integrated approaches can enhance the nutritional value of diets, reduce water usage, and provide a broader range of products, ensuring that both food quantity and quality are addressed.

Finally, policy frameworks and global cooperation are essential for supporting aquaculture as a driver of food security. Governments must create favorable policies that encourage sustainable practices, support smallholder aquaculture, and ensure equitable access to resources. International collaboration can help address challenges such as trade barriers, knowledge gaps, and shared environmental concerns, ensuring that aquaculture can contribute to global food security in a way that benefits all nations, particularly those in developing regions where aquaculture has the greatest potential for growth.

In conclusion, the pathways to global food security through aquaculture involve scaling production sustainably, innovating in feed, integrating systems, and implementing supportive policies. By focusing on these pathways, aquaculture can play a crucial role in feeding the world while preserving the planet's resources for future generations.